DJ Uncle Tiny (center) and Louis Jordan (second from right)
outside the Manor Plaza Hotel, 930 Fillmore Street, 1950s. *Steve Jackson Jr.*

L–R: Skippy Warren on bass, "Cowboy" on drums, Jerome Richardson, and Pony Poindexter, on stage at Bop City, 1950s. *Steve Jackson Jr.*

Celebrating a record release at a Fillmore diner, circa 1950s. *Steve Jackson Jr.*

Texas Playhouse patrons with Lottie "The Body," a local dance star (with blonde hair, third from the right), and Harlem Globetrotters star Goose Tatum (far right), 1950s.

Charles Sullivan (left), one of the most active promoters of African American music west of the Mississippi.
In the middle is Lionel Hampton wearing Wesley Johnson Sr.'s cowboy hat, 1950s.

Paul Gonsalves, saxophone player in Duke Ellington's band, with Flip Nunez
on piano, on stage at Bop City, 1950s. *Jerry Stoll*

HARLEM OF THE WEST ★ THE SAN FRANCISCO FILLMORE JAZZ ERA

by **ELIZABETH PEPIN** *and* **LEWIS WATTS**

CHRONICLE BOOKS
SAN FRANCISCO

*To my grandfather, Alfred Lewis Pepin Sr., a musician
who always wanted me to put together "a little girl's
band." And to my husband, David Silva, who's love makes
all things possible.* —E.P.

*To my parents, Lewis and Elvie Watts, whose lives were
affected by the great migration west during World War II,
as were the residents of the Fillmore.* —L.W.

Library of Congress Cataloging-in-Publication:
Pepin, Elizabeth.
Harlem of the West : the San Francisco Fillmore jazz era / by Elizabeth Pepin and Lewis Watts.
    p. cm.
Includes bibliographical references.
ISBN-10: 0-8118-4548-6
ISBN-13: 978-0-8118-4548-9
1. Fillmore (San Francisco, Calif.)—Social life and customs—20th century.
2. San Francisco (Calif.)—Social life and customs—20th century. 3. African Americans—California—San Francisco—Social life and customs—20th century.
4. African Americans—California—San Francisco—Intellectual life—20th century.
5. Jazz—California—San Francisco—History—20th century. 6. Nightclubs—California—San Francisco—History—20th century. 7. Fillmore (San Francisco, Calif.)—Intellectual life—20th century. 8. San Francisco (Calif.)—Intellectual life—20th century. 9. Fillmore (San Francisco, Calif.)—Biography. 10. San Francisco (Calif.)—Biography. I. Watts, Lewis, 1946– . II. Title.
F869.S36F55 2005
976.4'934—dc22

2005016619

Manufactured in China.
Designed by STRIPE [Sueda & Swanlund with Jeremy Landman], Los Angeles.

Distributed in Canada by Raincoast Books
9050 Shaughnessy Street
Vancouver, British Columbia V6P 6E5

10 9 8 7 6 5 4 3 2 1

Chronicle Books LLC
85 Second Street
San Francisco, California 94105

www.chroniclebooks.com

Photographs courtesy of the Eddie Alley family: pp. 34, 35; John and Frances Lynne Coppola collections: pp. 84, 85, 87, 127, 133; John Goddard collection: pp. 36, 113, 128, 129; Johnnie Ingram collection: pp. 44, 45, 46, 47 (articles); Frank Jackson collection: pp. 48, 49, 66, 80, 125 left, 140, 141, 149; Wesley Johnson Jr. collection: pp. 6, 7, 50, 51, 52, 53, 55, 59, 62, 63, 68, 82, 95, 96, 97, 98, 99, 100, 101, 102, 103, 104, 106, 107, 110, 111, 163, 182; Mike Mustaccha: p. 39; Elizabeth Pepin: pp. 32, 54, 74, 105; Red Powell/Reggie Pettus collection: pp. 12, 14 right, 17, 38, 59, 76, 77, 78, 79, 85, 109, 115, 116, 131, 132, 133, 134, 135, 136, 137, 140, 145, 147 top, 148, 151, 151, 171, 172 right, 175 right, 176, 178, 181; San Francisco Redevelopment Agency: pp. 33, 39 left, 42, 94, 166, 167, 168, 169, 170, 171; Yevette Stewart: p. 58; LaWanna Taylor: pp. 121, 122, 123, 124.
Photograph on this page by Susan Schwartzenberg.
Photograph on page 192 by Lewis Watts.
Front cover photograph by Steve Jackson Jr.
Back cover photograph by David Johnson.

The Steve Nakajo and Mayor Willie Brown interviews were conducted by Peter Stein during the filming of *Neighborhoods: The Hidden Cities of San Francisco: The Fillmore.* Excerpts from both interviews appear in the book courtesy of Peter Stein and KQED-TV, San Francisco.

Contents
· · · · ·

Photo collector Red Powell (right) and friends in front of his shoe-shine parlor, 1970s.

INTRODUCTION

—

Elizabeth Pepin

AND

Lewis Watts

· · · · ·

ELIZABETH'S STORY

The neighborhood was jumping. Block after block of ornate but slightly worn turn-of-the-century Victorians filled with all matters of fun. Everyone who was anyone could be found there, dressed to the nines, making the scene and strutting their stuff. Locals shaking off the working week drudgery could walk past Billie Holiday as she opened the door into the New Orleans Swing Club, or grab a stool next to T-Bone Walker chatting at the bar inside of the Texas Playhouse. Walk down the street and they might find John Coltrane, Chet Baker, or Dexter Gordon hanging out at Bop City, occasionally taking the stage to jam with the regulars. Back on the street, Dinah Washington's smooth vocals floated over the neighborhood as she practiced in her Booker T. Washington Hotel room.

During the musical heyday of the Fillmore District in the 1940s and 1950s, the area known as the Harlem of the West was a swinging place where you could leave your house Friday night and go from club to party to bar until the wee hours of Monday morning.

For more than two decades, music played nonstop in more than a dozen clubs where Young Turks from the neighborhood could mix with seasoned professionals and maybe even get a chance to jump onstage to prove their musical mettle. Filling out the streets in the twenty-square-block area were restaurants, pool halls, theaters, and stores, many of them owned and run by African Americans, Japanese Americans, and Filipino Americans. The entire neighborhood was a giant multicultural party throbbing with excitement and music.

The Fillmore has been commemorated in songs such as Lowell Fulson's "Fillmore Mess Around" and "San Francisco Blues"; *Rappin' with Ten Thousand Carabaos in the Dark*, a book of poetry by Al Robles; and in books like Maya Angelou's acclaimed novel *I Know Why the Caged Bird Sings*. But most people only know about the Fillmore because of its auditorium, made famous by Bill Graham in the late 1960s. Few are aware of its more important musical period in the decades preceding. The Fillmore was one of the few neighborhoods in

Fillmore Street, 1995.
An early effort to acknowledge the past. *Lewis Watts*

Right: The interior of Red's Shine Parlor, 1549 Fillmore Street, early 1970s. Some of the photos on the wall were given to Red by Wesley Johnson Sr. when the Club Flamingo/Texas Playhouse was closed and torn down by the Redevelopment Agency.

the Bay Area that people of color could go to for entertainment, during an era when only the most famous visiting African American musicians could play in the downtown clubs for strictly white audiences. After their gigs, the musicians had to return to the Fillmore hotels to sleep and Fillmore clubs to play and have fun.

Today, the neighborhood, remade under redevelopment in the 1960s and 1970s, offers few clues to its past. For serious researchers, little information is to be easily found in libraries and historical archives. More than seventy years after the first African American jazz nightclub opened in the neighborhood, the Fillmore's jazz, blues, and rhythm and blues musical history remains unwritten, a lapse that overlooks its contribution to the

history of jazz and African Americans in Northern California.

I was born in 1964 in the Bay Area, when redevelopment was going full force in the Fillmore. My first introduction to the neighborhood was in the late 1960s, from the backseat of the family car. We would pass through the Fillmore on our way to Sears Roebuck, at the top of Geary and Masonic. I recall being fascinated by the blocks of empty lots, wondering what had happened to all of the houses.

The 1970s for me were spent partially in the city and partially in the suburbs, dividing my time between divorced parents. I distinctly remember watching television one day in November 1978, when the program was interrupted to announce the tragedy in Guyana. I recognized the neighborhood where

reporters were now staking out the People's Temple headquarters, located just a few doors down from the unused Fillmore Auditorium. Passersby being interviewed looked bewildered, all of them trying to comprehend the horrible event.

Just a few years later, in 1981, finally able to drive, I found myself standing outside the very same building, drawn to the block by the punk rock shows held in several empty halls. Having eclectic musical tastes, my friends and I discovered that the neighborhood held a few small nightclubs and bars still featuring blues, R&B, and jazz. We would sometimes leave the punk shows to see Charles Brown at Dottie's Stardust Lounge or an unknown jazz combo at Jack's, decked out in our thrift-store clothes and funny haircuts. We were initially stared at, but once the few other patrons realized we too loved the music, we were accepted. I felt comfortable in the neighborhood, and when I struck out on my own, it felt natural to move to the area. It seemed that The Fillmore was always to be in my life.

In 1986 I was employed by Bill Graham Presents as day manager and historian of the Fillmore Auditorium. Part of my job was to research and write a short booklet on the history of the building. I was given only a few clues, among them that the auditorium had been an R&B nightclub before Bill began booking shows there at the end of 1965 and that the side of the building had the name "Majestic Hall" painted in fading white old-fashioned letters on the deep red bricks.

I found from a trip to the San Francisco Public Library that little had been written on the neighborhood, just a few articles and mentions in San Francisco history books. Therefore, I had to dig deeper. Six months of following up on leads from the articles, digging in city files, tracking down former residents via letters and phone calls—and just plain walking up to people I met in the neighborhood—turned up a few dozen old photos, concert posters, and a written patchwork history of the building. The more intriguing story was the one I was uncovering about the neighborhood.

The empty lots and nearly deserted streets had, for more than half a century, been a vibrant, thriving multicultural community filled with shops, restaurants, and entertainment. The Fillmore's theaters drew people from all over the world to play on their stages. At a nightclub a famous movie star banged away on the bongos, accompanying a local jazz band. A small girl with a powerful voice won a neighborhood talent show and in less than twenty-four hours found herself whisked away to Los Angeles to begin a recording career that spanned decades. A seventeen-year-old saxophone player jammed with his musical hero on a stage filled with musical heroes. And nearly all of it had been wiped away by urban renewal.

The answer to my childhood mystery of the empty lots was finally solved. I fell in love with the Fillmore—and became obsessed.

In my free time, I buried myself in the repository of every city records office I could think of and the public library's newspaper microfilm collection. I also began walking into the few businesses left on Fillmore Street. One, a shoe-shine parlor across from the Fillmore Auditorium, fascinated me with its wall-to-wall photo gallery of R&B and jazz musicians, neighborhood scenes, and even a classic portrait of John F. Kennedy. The owner, a small, older African American man, refused to talk with me and kicked me out after a few minutes. I later found out that the owner's name was Red and that he had been running his shoe-shine parlor for several decades. I suspected he could be a trove of neighborhood information, so I stopped by every so often, hoping he would say more than a few words to me. But it was not to be. I left San Francisco in 1989 to live in London for several years, and when I returned in 1992, he and his shop were no longer there.

One night in the late 1980s, after leaving the Fillmore Auditorium, I saw a group of old men standing outside the shoe-shine parlor, singing 1950s doo-wop hits a capella and drinking Colt 45s on the otherwise deserted street. The rich vocals of the quartet bounced off the entryway's chipped ceramic tiles, filling the block with sound. Illumination from the traffic lights reflecting off the wet asphalt spotlit their faces, as if the singers were on a stage. I stood there for more than an hour, mesmerized, brought back to a time when groups like this practiced on every corner of the neighborhood, getting ready for the weekly talent show held at the Ellis Theater and a chance to win a grand prize of $50.

People I met in the neighborhood began sharing their stories with me, bringing out photographs not seen in decades. Their faces were bright with memories as they recalled the scenes captured in black-and-white. After a while, I no longer saw the Fillmore of the 1990s, with its faceless modern buildings and vacant lots, but envisioned the more vivid, vibrant Fillmore of the 1940s, with its crowded streets lined with beautiful but decaying Victorians bustling with people and businesses. These photos and the stories that accompanied them brought the Fillmore to life for me. I could not believe that something so magical could vanish with hardly a trace within just a few decades.

LEWIS'S STORY

I first came to San Francisco in 1964, and I had the chance to visit the Fillmore at the end of its heyday. Some of the clubs still remained, and on a Saturday night, the streets were filled with activity. I was vaguely aware of urban renewal, but I had little idea of the neighborhood's history, other than a general knowledge about the great African American migration west during World War II. Indeed, my own Southern-born parents ended up in the West when my father was discharged from the army in Washington State. By 1990 I was a photographer, and I began looking at the Fillmore as a part of my general interest in a visual examination of history and contemporary experience in African American communities. Walking through the neighborhood, I also came across Red's shoe-shine parlor across from the Fillmore Auditorium. I went in and inquired about photographing the gallery on the walls that represented many who had lived and performed in the Fillmore. The owner of the shop, Elgin "Red" Powell, said that he was busy but that I might come back another time to talk about it. A few months passed, and when I returned, Red's shop was empty, and there was no trace of the pictures. No one in the neighborhood seemed to know what happened to Red and the photos in his shop. I was afraid that this valuable collection of history was lost. I continued to ask after its whereabouts for years.

In 1996 I was doing research for a report on the cultural past of the Fillmore, and I

Lewis Watts lecturing during the neighborhood history walk, 2003. *Bill Stender*

Left: Reggie Pettus in front of rescued photographs, New Chicago Barber Shop, Fillmore Street, 2005. *Lewis Watts*

again asked around the neighborhood about Red and his photographs. When I went into the New Chicago Barber Shop, across the street from Red's parlor, and asked one of the barbers, Reggie Pettus, I was thrilled by his response: "They are in my back room."

Reggie filled in the blanks about what had happened. Red Powell had a stroke not long after we met in the early 1990s, lost his lease, and died soon afterward. When the parlor closed, everything was taken from the walls and was about to be tossed into a dumpster by the landlord. Reggie rescued the photographs and memorabilia and had kept the materials ever since.

Reggie was happy to let me go through the boxes. This discovery began a period of intense activity for me as an archivist. Many of the images had aged badly, and, with

Reggie's blessing, I began digitally restoring them. I used Red's collection in a report on the neighborhood and curated an exhibition that was first displayed outside Mayor Willie Brown's office in City Hall, and later in the San Francisco Art Commission Gallery across the street.

The photographs and artifacts from the original collection, along with a growing body of work Elizabeth and I have found over the past fifteen years, are a remarkable reflection of history, informally documented. The images tell stories, raise questions, and capture the incredible joy and sense of style conveyed to us in our talks with people about the period. We are fortunate that many of the clubs employed photographers to shoot the performers, employees, and patrons. The collections are also a tribute to the individuals who took the time and energy to save them.

This page: Fillmore installation panels, Fillmore Street, 2003. *Lewis Watts*

Drawing of Elgin "Red" Powell, owner of Red's Shine Parlor.

"Fillmore Blue" installation on Fillmore Street by artist Mildred Howard, 2004. *Lewis Watts*

The ever-expanding archive has been used in documentary films (including the KQED production *The Fillmore*, for which Elizabeth was associate producer), Web sites, a number of publications, and a storefront installation that we helped curate on Fillmore Street in the very location of many of the clubs. It continues to be an honor and inspiration to see and work with the materials we have found. I've talked to older residents who go by the installation every day because it reminds them of a period they say was the best in their lives.

OUR STORY

When we finally met each other in 1998, while Elizabeth was doing research for a PBS documentary on the Fillmore neighborhood, we realized that we had been on the same path for years. Once she was finished working on the film, Elizabeth planned to resume her history research and begin interviewing people with the intention of creating a book.

Lewis had been contemplating the same idea, so we decided to join forces and focus on the Fillmore's vibrant music scene, with Elizabeth interviewing and writing, and Lewis organizing the photo collections and painstakingly repairing the damaged images in order to prepare them for publication.

These pages capture a joyful, exciting time in San Francisco's history through more than two hundred rare images, many of them unpublished until now. Firsthand accounts from musicians, nightclub patrons, and former residents of the Fillmore bring the images to life, taking you through the city's premier historic Black neighborhood. Both reveal a momentous but nearly forgotten part of San Francisco's history and the country's African American musical heritage.

This book is meant to be a slice of life, not a completist's history nor an analysis of events. Due to space constraints, many worthy people from the neighborhood have been left

out. This does not detract from the one idea that everyone agrees upon: The Fillmore was a magical place. We hope you fall in love with this neighborhood, as we have.

We are grateful that photographers, their families, and collectors have shared with us the images and memorabilia that capture the magic of the Fillmore. Smaller holdings featured in the book include the work of the famous late jazz photographer Jerry Stoll; the collections of Wesley Johnson Jr., the son of a Fillmore nightclub owner; memorabilia from Yevette Stewart, the daughter of a Fillmore jazz musician; the collections of jazz musicians Frank Jackson, John Coppola, Francis Lynne, and Johnnie Ingram; and photographs from Lawanna Taylor, the daughter of Fillmore nightclub owners; the San Francisco Redevelopment Agency, Bill Sender and John Goddard, owner of Village Music in Mill Valley, California.

Jerry Stoll, self-portrait.

Portrait of
Ricardo Alvarado,
1950s.

THE PHOTOGRAPHERS

We are also delighted to highlight several large collections from the Fillmore, including the one belonging to Red Powell/Reggie Pettus. Over the course of several decades, Red Powell's shoe-shine parlor had several locations, the last being at 1549 Fillmore Street, across from the Fillmore Auditorium. His shop was more than a place to get a shoe shine. It was a small impromptu community and history center, its walls covered with photographs of the many famous people who had passed through Red's life, as well as scenes from the neighborhood.

Like Red, Reggie Pettus, who rescued Red's collection and stored it in his barbershop, is an archivist. In the Black community, the barbershop has traditionally been the place where local history and lore are collected in conversations and on the walls. With the help of Lewis Watts, Reggie began displaying the photos in galleries and other locations in the neighborhood. Many of the photos can be seen on the walls of his New Chicago Barber

Shop, 1551 Fillmore Street, across the street from their former home.

Lewis met the daughter of Filipino photographer Ricardo Ocreto Alvarado (1914–1976) during an exhibit at the San Francisco Public Library. Alvarado arrived in California in 1928 as a fourteen-year-old in the first wave of Filipino immigrants, known as the Manong generation. Working as a janitor and houseboy, he enlisted in the U.S. Army's First Filipino Infantry Regiment in 1942 and later became a civilian cook at San Francisco's Letterman Army Hospital. After World War II, with view camera in hand, Alvarado began recording Filipino community life. Many of his photographs were taken in the Fillmore District, where he lived. In 1959 Alvarado ended his work in photography and returned to the Philippines to marry Norberta Magallanes. They had two children. When he died of

leukemia in 1976, Alvarado left a collection of nearly three thousand rare photographs, a vital portrait of early Filipino and ethnic American life in California. His daughter Janet is curator of the Alvarado collection.

An exhibition of Alvarado's work, *Through My Father's Eyes: The Filipino American Photographs of Ricardo Ocreto Alvarado (1914–1976)*, premiered at the Smithsonian Institution's National Museum of American History, Behring Center Photo Documentary Gallery, in November 2002. When the exhibition closed, SITES (Smithsonian Institution Traveling Exhibition Service) sent it on a fifteen-city national tour through 2006. More information about the collection is available at www.thealvaradoproject.org.

One of Elizabeth's jobs while working on the PBS Fillmore documentary was to find images of the neighborhood. The cache that I had unearthed in my previous research was insufficient to cover an hour-long film, so I once again took to the streets in hope of finding people who could help. An uneventful cab ride to the Fillmore Auditorium turned incredible when the cab driver mentioned that he used to roller skate in the building as a kid. I told him about the film project I was working on and asked if he had any photographs or footage. He said he didn't, but he used to play cards with an African American photographer who had a huge collection of neighborhood shots. He said he'd try to track the guy down for me, and I gave him my contact information.

Steve Jackson Jr., self-portrait,
circa 1950s.

Several weeks went by without a phone call, and I was growing desperate. Finally, after nearly a month, the cab driver called, apologizing for the long delay, and said that he had finally tracked the gentleman down, and he lived in Hunters Point. I eagerly dialed the phone number given to me and, much to my delight, was soon on my way to visit Steve Jackson Jr. Over the course of the following year, I had the pleasure to hang out with Steve in his garage "office," which was filled with photographs, negatives, dozens of cameras, and boxes of accessories. Each time, Jackson would sit me down at the rickety folding card table in the middle of the cement floor,

and he would hand me a large plastic glass of white wine that he expected me to drink before he would begin pulling out his photographs. I could tell my slow drinking habits disappointed him, but he was still happy to show me his work, and, although it had been decades, he could recall the circumstances that led to many of the photos. After a few hours, I'd reluctantly leave the garage, hungry to see more photographs but too woozy from the wine to sit any longer. I'd slowly drive home and head straight to bed for a nap!

Steve Jackson Jr. (1923–1999) was born and raised in Houston, Texas, where he went to a private school and learned photography.

He soon discovered that he enjoyed doing "as is" photography rather than set-up portraits. During World War II, Jackson was stationed in Pittsburg, California, and fell in love with the Bay Area, then once discharged, he returned to Texas. In 1951 Jackson left Houston with his new wife to come to San Francisco in search of a better life, free of the degradations and humiliation of Jim Crow. His wife, Mary, decided to enroll in beauty college, where she met Leola Edwards. The women became fast friends. Leola mentioned that her husband, Jimbo, owned a nightclub where jazz singers and musicians from all over the world performed, and that the two men should meet. Edwards and Jackson, who looked enough alike that people thought they were brothers, hit it off immediately. Jackson began shooting photos inside the famous club, using both 4×5 and 220 cameras. He would develop the film on the spot, in a darkroom he had set up in Bop City. Jackson and Edwards's partnership, which began in 1952 and spanned almost thirty years, created an incredible photographic history of the Fillmore. Jackson was also a photographer for the *Sun-Reporter* newspaper.

David Johnson has been an established Bay Area photographer for more than five decades. Born in 1926 in Jacksonville, Florida, he first came to San Francisco when he shipped out with the U.S. Navy during World War II. He returned in 1946, becoming a pioneer as a photographer and a community member. He was the first African American student in Ansel Adams's photographic class at the California School of Fine Arts (now the San Francisco Art Institute) and also studied with renowned photographers Minor White and Imogen Cunningham. Johnson later had a photography studio in the Fillmore, and his work has appeared in many exhibitions.

Johnson still resides in San Francisco and continues to photograph the Fillmore. I met him while working on the Fillmore documentary, after his son Michael told me about his father's work. Of all the photographers in the book, Johnson is the only one still living and able to share his story with me.

David Johnson's Story

I fell in love with photography at age twelve. I was very interested in music, but my foster mother didn't appreciate music practice in her house, and she wanted me to find something else to do. I happened to win a small camera in a contest and began snapping photos. When I started seeing the results, I was fascinated. I now had a hobby that didn't create any noise!

In my late teens, I registered for the draft and joined the navy. After four weeks of training in San Francisco, which took place at the Tanforan Racetrack out by the San Francisco Airport, I remember being on liberty and ending up on Seventh Street, near Market, where the Greyhound Bus Station was for many years. I got over to Market Street and asked someone, "Where are the Black people?" So this gentleman told me, and I remember this very well, "You get on the B car, and you tell them to put you off on Fillmore. Fillmore and Geary."

I had never heard of Fillmore before. So I landed on Fillmore and Geary, the very same spot that, much later in my life, I was to photograph. I walked up and down the streets, which were very crowded. People were hustling and trying to run a game on me or sell me something because I was a sailor and they thought I had money. There were lots of bars open. Lots going on. I was seventeen years old.

After the war, I returned to Jacksonville and decided I wanted to study photography. There was nothing else that excited me as much as the magic of getting a picture out of the little box. But there wasn't any place in Florida to study, so I wasn't sure what to do. Browsing through an issue of *Popular Photography,* I saw a small article announcing that Ansel Adams was setting up a photography department at the California School of Fine Arts in San Francisco. I wanted to return to California, so I wrote directly to Ansel, telling him I wanted to come to San Francisco and study photography, but I wanted to make it clear that I was a Negro. I didn't want to come all that way and have them not know who I was. Back then, all your decisions were made around race, and they still are, to a certain extent.

Ansel Adams answered me right away via telegram. He said that it didn't matter if I was a Negro, and if I wanted to study photography there, that was fine. Funny thing was, I knew nothing of Ansel Adams. But I knew the school was in San Francisco, and that was good enough for me.

I hopped on a segregated train at the Jacksonville depot and headed for San Francisco. Ansel had written that a gentleman named Minor White would meet me when I arrived, and he knew I was to live at Ansel's house until I found a place to live. I think they were just excited a Black was going to come three thousand miles to be in their school.

I arrived on August 27, 1946, and Minor and I took the B car all the way out to Sea Cliff, to 121 Twenty-fourth Avenue, where Ansel lived. Also living there was Ruth-Marion Baruch, Pirkle Jones, and several other photographers.

The next day we went to 800 Chestnut Street, where the school was, and I sat in a room with all these people. My association with white people changed dramatically at that point, because I would never have been sitting in a room in 1944 with a group of white students in Jacksonville or anywhere in the South. It was a brand-new experience and also kind of a culture shock. I felt a sense of inferiority, and I kept thinking to myself, How you going to manage? The language they were using when they started to look at photographs had terms I never heard of before. I didn't know what they were talking about. But they accepted me. I wasn't enough of a threat, and I was the youngest person in the class.

When Ansel and I finally met, we shook hands and he told me he was glad I was there, so that was reassuring. I learned a lot. Since I lived in his house, I also worked in his darkroom. We had a great time, and he showed me different things to do. Eventually I moved out and rented a room in the Fillmore, but I'd still come over to get private lessons from Minor. As a result of those sessions, I became an excellent printer.

Eventually, I began running out of money, so I went to Mt. Zion hospital, and a woman named Mrs. Richter—I'll never forget her—was so impressed there was this Black kid studying photography that she gave me a job right away in the kitchen. That's when I began to meet people like Terry Francois and Jamie Kennedy. They were the early leadership of African Americans emerging in the city.

At the same time, I began meeting people interested in having photographs of the Black community. I met Ed Howden, head of the Council for Civic Unity, an organization set up to improve relations between the races, who asked me if I had photographed the Fillmore.

I asked him, "Where's the Fillmore?" He said, "Where do you live?" I told him I lived between Sutter and Bush Streets, and he said, "You live in the Fillmore, and there are a lot of social problems there you should be capturing." So I did. The neighborhood became significant in my photographic life. I got a very large camera and began to do what I didn't perceive at the time—documentary photography. It was 1947, so I had enough skills. The *Sun-Reporter* newspaper was just emerging, and I became the staff reporter. Some of my more well-known photos, like Eartha Kitt, were as a result of going out on assignment for the newspaper.

As I became friends with Ed, we began to talk about the social issues in San Francisco, and I started to make the connection—that the photographs I was taking in the slum

housing had a direct relationship with what was going on downtown. San Francisco wanted to have this facade that it was a liberal city and would always point to those guys down South, that they were the bigots. But the people in San Francisco were the worst bigots of all because they were hiding behind a facade of liberalism.

I met my wife while working at Mt. Zion, and we married and started having kids. I got a job at the post office but was still taking photographs. I found a storefront with a three-bedroom apartment in back in the Fillmore and rented it. I had a darkroom built and created a little reception area in front and put my sign up, which said Johnson Studio. Business that first year was great, but shooting photos all day and working at the post office at night was beginning to take its toll on me. So I closed the studio, but I continued to shoot photographs. The neighborhood. The rise of Willie Brown. The Civil Rights Movement in San Francisco. I felt like I was in "the zone"—that I was able to capture really powerful images. It was probably my most productive time.

L-R: Photographer David Johnson and John Templeton in front of Marcus Books, 2003. The building originally was on Post Street and housed Bop City. It was moved to Fillmore Street during Redevelopment.

Portrait of a Fillmore resident, 1950s. *Ricardo Alvarado*

A neighborhood family celebrating Thanksgiving, circa 1940s. *Ricardo Alvarado*

Party in a Fillmore flat, 1940s. *Ricardo Alvarado*

Eartha Kitt with neighborhood children, 1950s. *David Johnson*

Fillmore Street Cleaners, circa 1950s. Many Fillmore businesses were owned and run by
African Americans in the 1950s and '60s. *David Johnson*

The Dog House Bar, 1692 Fillmore Street, late 1940s. *David Johnson*

Chapter 1

The NEIGHBORHOOD

THE FILLMORE, JAPANTOWN, THE WESTERN ADDITION, NIHONMACHI, the 'MO:

Bird's-eye view of Fillmore Street, looking south toward Post Street and Geary Street, late 1940s. The Fillmore Auditorium is on the right in the distance, with Temple Beth Israel next to it on the right. The temple burned down in the late 1980s, nearly taking the Fillmore Auditorium with it.
David Johnson

Many names have been used for the neighborhood located just west of San Francisco's City Hall. The area became internationally known in the late 1960s for its auditorium, which showcased the best of the era's musical talent and launched the career of concert promoter Bill Graham. While the Fillmore Auditorium might be famous, the neighborhood and its history of more than 130 years are largely unfamiliar.

By the 1880s, San Francisco was a crowded metropolis that lacked enough housing to meet the demands of the continuously expanding population. City officials, needing to alleviate some of the congestion, decided to expand the street grid to include the area west of City Hall. They called the hundreds of new square blocks the Western Addition and began encouraging home building in the area. A multitude of large Victorian mansions began to spring up, many of them among the most ornate in the city. Fillmore Street, which ran north-south through the middle of the neighborhood and carried a streetcar, became the commercial district. Residents began referring to the twenty square blocks around the street as "The Fillmore."

At first, the Fillmore was mainly white, settled by European and Jewish home owners. As the neighborhood grew, several large synagogues were built in the area, and restaurants, grocery stores, and dry good stores sprang up along Fillmore Street. By the late 1890s, Japanese immigrants began to move in and establish shops around Post Street near Fillmore Street, instead of the more popular Japanese area in Chinatown. Several African American families also moved into the area.

The earthquake and fire of April 1906 changed the course of the city forever. With most of downtown in ruins, the closest area left relatively untouched happened to be the Fillmore. The first streetcar to begin operating again went down Fillmore Street. Within days, City Hall, most of the newspapers, and many

of the major department stores relocated to the neighborhood, setting up shop and erecting makeshift hand-painted signs on the Victorians along Fillmore and nearby side streets. The Fillmore became San Francisco's downtown, financial center, and seat of government. To accommodate the huge number of homeless, many of the large Victorian homes in the surrounding area were turned into boardinghouses. People from all over the city flocked to the Fillmore, transforming the once quiet community into a noisy, bustling urban center.

Within a few years after the earthquake, the neighborhood became a melting pot. Japanese Americans living in Chinatown before the earthquake moved to the Fillmore around the few Japanese-owned businesses already in the neighborhood, and the area became known as Nihonmachi (Japantown). Filipinos, Mexicans, African Americans, and Russians joined the Japanese Americans and the Jewish population. With its integrated schools and some integrated businesses, the Fillmore soon had a reputation as one of the most diverse neighborhoods west of the Mississippi.

Although the government offices and many of the major stores returned to downtown once it was rebuilt, the Fillmore continued to attract patrons to its many fine restaurants and good Jewish delis and bakeries. Merchants belonging to the Fillmore Street Improvement Association worried, however, that business was falling off. To lure patrons back to the neighborhood, the group

put up fourteen brightly lit steel arches over each Fillmore Street intersection, and the street soon became known, according to a newspaper account at the time, as "the most highly illuminated thoroughfare in America."

The Fillmore also began reinventing itself as an entertainment center. The National Hall, built in 1907 at the corner of Steiner and Post, regularly featured the young Al Jolson, who sang there for $60 a week. The Fillmore Chutes, one of the first amusement parks west of City Hall, opened on a square block bounded by Fillmore, Turk, Eddy, and Webster streets in 1909. Dreamland Rink, 1725 Steiner at Post Street, was famous for its boxing and wrestling matches. The Majestic Hall, later known as the Majestic Ballroom and the Fillmore Auditorium, was built in 1910 by Emma Gates Butler and her two daughters. Butler commissioned James W. and Merritt Reid, popular architects who also designed many other buildings in the city, among them the Fairmont Hotel, Embassy Theater, and First Congregational Church. The hall became a popular place for dances and balls, although it remained segregated until the 1950s.

African Americans had been living in the Fillmore District since before the earthquake, but their numbers were quite small. Racism in employment and a ban on nonwhites by nearly all labor unions kept San Francisco's Black population from growing, in contrast to Oakland, which had a robust African American community, mainly due to its proximity to the railroad. In the decade prior to the

The Majestic Hall, Geary at Fillmore, 1914. The lit steel
arches with the glass balls suspended in the middle were placed
at intersections along Fillmore Street to attract shoppers to the
district. The lights led several newspapers at the time to declare
Fillmore Street "the most illuminated street in America."

war, the African American population of San Francisco numbered just 4,846, most of them living in the Fillmore due to racial covenants in real estate deeds, which restricted where they could live and own property.

While the neighborhood was more tolerant than the rest of the city, and certainly the rest of the country, people of color still felt the sting of racism within the Fillmore. In the 1920s, according to Albert S. Broussard in his book *Black San Francisco: The Struggle for Racial Equality in the West, 1900–1954*, the area's Black community came together to buy a building on Divisadero Street to house the city's first African American community center, which they named after Booker T. Washington. Some white residents were not happy about it, and although they were unable to stop the purchase, they managed to eventually buy the loan from the bank and tried to foreclose on the property when the group fell behind on one payment. The community had just weeks to come up with the money, which they miraculously did after soliciting funds by going door to door and holding nonstop fund-raisers such as bake sales. Additionally, up until the 1940s, people of color were still restricted from patronizing some Fillmore stores and most bars, restaurants, and nightclubs.

World War II dramatically changed the face of the Fillmore. By the 1950 census, San Francisco's Black population had exploded to 42,520, due to the many African Americans from the South who were encouraged to come to the West Coast to work in the shipyards. The Western Addition, with the sudden removal of the Japanese and Japanese American population to relocation camps and its small but established population of African Americans, naturally drew the newcomers. This caused some tension between the established Black community and the new transplants, who, according to Broussard, were seen as brash and too "country." However, the increase in the community created a need for services, and soon a thriving district of Black-run nightclubs, shops, and restaurants lined the streets of the Fillmore.

Earl WATKINS

Watkins was born in the Fillmore on January 29, 1920, in a rooming house that still exists on Sutter Street, between Broderick and Baker. His family moved to a succession of flats, each one closer to Fillmore Street. As a teenager, he became a regular on drums at local clubs. He was also a member of the Five Knights of Rhythm and played and made recordings with Earl Hines and Dizzy Gillespie. Watkins lives in Oakland and continues to play jazz in clubs and for social occasions.

The busy corner of Geary and Fillmore, February 1952. Thom McCann and Darnells are on the 1600 block of Fillmore. The image was taken by the San Francisco Redevelopment Agency, who painstakingly photographed, numbered, and catalogued each building in the Fillmore, noting on each file if the structure was worth saving. Unfortunately, most were deemed unworthy and later torn down, as was the case with all the buildings in this photo.

EARL WATKINS: My father was a World War I veteran from Alabama, and, when he got out of the service, he decided that the racial climate was much better in San Francisco, even though it wasn't the best. African Americans had a lot of freedom in San Francisco, especially on the Barbary Coast. It was going full blast, and Blacks owned many of the clubs.

My mother played piano and was classically trained, and my dad played the ukulele and would sing. That is what we did in our home. My mother wanted to teach me piano, but I wanted to go out and play. I still kick myself a thousand times for having missed that opportunity. When I was a teen, I went to a dance and became fascinated by the drummer because he had different things going on—each appendage was doing something different.

So I asked him how he did it, and he asked if I'd like to learn. I said I would, so he gave me the address to his house, which was in the neighborhood, and said he'd see me the next day to see if I had talent. He put on a record and played along with it, and then said, "Let's see if you can follow the record." So I sat down, and I could keep time and stay with the record. That was my start. I went there every week for free lessons.

I was always on Fillmore. It was bustling because after the 1906 earthquake Fillmore Street was the main business district. You had electrical shops, hardware stores, restaurants, bars, dress shops, beauty parlors. Store to store, bumper to bumper so to speak. At that time, before the war, they were white owned. The restaurants and grocery stores, naturally, welcomed you. But the other places, such as the bars and nightclubs, did not. The Japanese welcomed you—more than welcomed you—not only in their restaurants but also in their hotels and rooming houses.

Vernon ALLEY

Bassist Vernon Alley, Eddie's younger brother, was born in 1916, when the family lived in Winnemucca, Nevada, before moving to San Francisco. He was an all-star fullback and linebacker in high school, where he began his musical career as a clarinetist, soon switching to bass. He began playing in the Wes Peoples Band and with Saunders King. In 1939, Lionel Hampton discovered Vernon at a Fillmore club and brought him on tour. He was also a member of the Count Basie Band, which resulted in a film appearance. He later returned to the Fillmore and had a radio show on KLOK, *Vernon's Alley,* and a TV program on KPIX, *Nipper's Song Shop.* He was also musical director of the Blackhawk Jazz Club on Hyde Street and for *The Merv Griffin Show* during San Francisco tapings. Vernon Alley played on dozens of recordings. He passed away in 2004.

Eddie and Dorothy Alley just after they were married, San Francisco, 1939.

The ALLEY FAMILY

Eddie Alley was handed a drum at a school music session and never stopped playing. Born on December 19, 1910, in Minneapolis, he came to San Francisco with his family in the 1920s. They moved to the Fillmore District in 1928. His band, with singer Sweetie Mitchell, played steadily for more than two decades. His wife of more than sixty years, Dorothy, grew up in the Fillmore and, for a short time, worked as a waitress at the Club Flamingo/Texas Playhouse. Their son Philip, born August 31, 1940, was spoon-fed jazz from an early age and began sneaking into Fillmore clubs in his early teens. All three live in San Francisco.

Eddie and Dorothy Alley at the Musician's Hall, 2004

L–R: Unknown, Billy Eckstein, Teddy Edwards, Ernie Lewis, and Vernon Alley, circa early 1950s.

Eddie Alley behind his drum kit, 1950s. Eddie and
his brother Vernon were among the more well-known musicians
who were born and raised in San Francisco.

EDDIE ALLEY: In 1928 we moved from Potrero Hill to the Fillmore District. It was a wonderful district, too. Very integrated. Black people were in the Fillmore before the war and were used to being integrated. We didn't encounter prejudice there at all, hardly. But the prejudice would come if we looked for work. When I got out of high school, I couldn't get a job on the streetcars. I couldn't get a job in department stores. I couldn't get a job any-place. So I got a job as a redcap down on Third Street and Townsend. In those days, they didn't even pay a salary— we worked for tips only. I was also playing little dances in the Fillmore, mainly at the Booker T. Washington Community Center on Divisadero. Earl Watkins played there, too.

In 1930s, I got a job at Topsy's Roost, a restaurant and dance hall down at Playland at the Beach amusement park. I was a busboy, but I liked music so much I talked the manager into letting me play the drums along with phonograph records until the band came on at 9 P.M. The musicians' union found out and said I had to join the union. So I went to a school of music, learned how to read and improv, and then went down to the union, took my examination, and passed.

I began playing in a band with Wes Peoples, a saxophonist. He started me out in music more than anybody. He'd get jobs and take me with him, so I began playing quite a bit. We got $7 a day, but I thought it was great. I loved it. Later on I began to play with different guys and started to form my own ideas about music. I began playing ballads and different types of music. More commercial.

Sugar Pie
DESANTO

Born October 16, 1935, and raised in the Fillmore, DeSanto began singing at an early age, along with her cousin, Etta James. She was discovered in her early teens by Johnny Otis while singing at a Fillmore talent show at the Ellis Theater. Within a few days, she was in Los Angeles recording her first record. DeSanto continues to record and perform internationally, returning home to Oakland whenever she can.

Sugar Pie DeSanto on stage at the Veterans Hall in Redwood City, 1958.

SUGAR PIE DESANTO: 1131 Buchanan Street. The cross street was Webster. I'll never forget it. That was my childhood. We were a mixed product. Every race and religion you could think of. We all lived in the neighborhood and were all good friends.

My father was Filipino, and my mother was Black. There were ten of us: six brothers and four sisters. My mother was a concert pianist and taught me a lot of what I know today about ballads. I used to sing with her and she'd play the piano. I had a brother that went to Julliard and ended up in jazz, and another brother who has his own band, Domingo and Friends.

The neighborhood was very music-oriented, of course. You could walk down Fillmore Street and see all kinds of clubs lined up one behind the other, and the musicians could gig all the time. I mean, just music out of the doors, windows, people's houses. It was just music, music, music. There would be doo-wop groups on the street. Standing on the corner, maybe by one of the theaters or over by the bowling alley, there would be a little group of neighborhood kids in the street, singing and going crazy. Just like me and Etta James, my cousin. She was tight with my sister, who was in her group, the Peaches. We all used to get together on my porch and sing.

Flip Wilson would come home and eat with my family at my table. He would just hang around, and we'd see him in the streets and come home to eat. We'd break beans together. He was just starting his comedy.

ARMANDO P. RENDON: Filipinos began coming to San Francisco in the 1910s and '20s. When they got here, they would either move to Kearny Street, downtown, or to the Fillmore. I don't know why. All the Filipino businesses in the Fillmore were on Geary, between Laguna and Webster Streets. That was when Geary was a regular two-lane street, not like it is today. The place I recall the most was a Filipino barbershop and a pool hall, located on Geary near Buchanan Street, and in spaces that were side by side, but with a door cut into the wall, so that people could go back and forth. As a teen, I would go get my haircut and then go play pool with my friends. The crowd was mainly Filipino. A lot of the Filipino old timers would hang out there and reminisce. They were natty dressers, good dancers, and very good pool players. But they were also hard working and very family-oriented men.

The Fillmore during the '40s and '50s was fabulous. A great place to raise kids. The neighborhood was very mixed, and we didn't have any racially motivated outbreaks of violence. I feel very fortunate to have grown up in a multi-cultural environment. I never experienced any racism until I entered the banking field in the early 1960s. That was the first time I felt white racism against me.

Painting of Willie Brown, which hangs in the
New Chicago Barber Shop.

Willie BROWN

Former San Francisco Mayor Willie Brown
was born in Minneola, Texas, and arrived in
San Francisco in August 1951. He earned a
degree in political science from San Francisco
State University, working his way through
college as a doorman, janitor, and shoe
salesman. He then went on to get a degree
from Hastings Law School. After losing the
Democratic primary in his first bid for the
State Assembly in 1962, Brown regrouped
for a decisive victory in 1964. He went on to
become Speaker of the Assembly, and, later,
Mayor of San Francisco from 1996 to 2003.
He continues to live in San Francisco.

WILLIE BROWN: The first place I lived in when I came to
San Francisco was the Western Addition. From the house,
I would wander all over the city, but particularly all over
the Fillmore. It was a joy for a kid like me to see the magic
kingdom, and that's how I thought San Francisco really
was. The Victorians looked like gingerbread houses.
You can imagine, a little kid from Texas, seeing all these
incredible structures.

The Fillmore was a Black community: Black barber-
shops, barbecue pits, stores that were as important as
the ones in Union Square except they carried goods that
Blacks would primarily purchase. I worked at Kaufman's
Shoe Store at 1607 Fillmore, so I lived, worked, and played
in the neighborhood. It was my playground.

In the evening, you would walk down the same streets
looking for parties. People would get dressed to kill. You
saw great peacocks. Stacey Adams shoes with the white
strings showing that had been cleaned up with Clorox.
Diamond stick pins. Satin ties and long coats. Great
looking jewelry on the women. Fur coats—there was no
such thing as an endangered species. Believe me, you
didn't go out in jeans and sneakers. You had to be dressed.
It was a great, great time. I would say it was Harlem. And
I say that because Sammy Davis Jr., Duke Ellington, Ella
Fitzgerald, Miles Davis, they all fell into San Francisco like
the artists that I read about would fall into New York. It
was the way many people wrote about the renaissance in
Harlem. That was what Fillmore Street was like in those
days. It had to be the closest thing to Harlem outside of
New York.

GallenKamp shoe store, 1698 Fillmore Street, on the corner of Post looking north toward Sutter Street, February 1952. Although newspapers at this time characterized the neighborhood as a slum, residents saw a busy shopping district, filled with thriving stores, restaurants, and nightclubs.

Armando P. RENDON

Armando Rendon's father came from the Philippines in the early 1920s, and his mother from Guatemala in 1929. The couple met in San Francisco's Fillmore District, married, and settled in a house on Bush and Octavia Streets, where their son, Armando, was born in October 1933. The family moved to several other houses in the Fillmore before settling at 682 Olive Street, a small street that ran between Laguna and Buchanan. The Rendons lived in the home until Armando was eighteen, when the Redevelopment Agency bought the building and evicted the tenants. They were the last family to move. Armando continues to live in San Francisco.

Steve NAKAJO

Steve Nakajo was born in Salt Lake City, Utah, and moved to San Francisco's Japantown in 1956. In the late 1960s, he became a community activist, and he organized the first Nihonmachi Street Fair in Japantown in 1972. Nakajo founded and continues to be executive director of Kimochi, Inc., a multiservice senior center providing a variety of services targeting Japanese seniors and their families, located in the heart of Japantown. He continues to live in the Bay Area.

STEVE NAKAJO: South Park (in the South of Market neighborhood) was the first Japantown in San Francisco. The second was on Grant Avenue, right in the heart of Chinatown. The third one, the one I grew up in, was in the Western Addition. Japantown was created because Japanese immigrants had to come together because of all the racist laws that restricted them and prevented them from owning property. When faced with this, you come together to create a community. You use your culture as a tool to endure discrimination. What's amazing to me is that in spite of this, there was such a strong desire to adopt this country. To participate in being in America.

When I was growing up, in the mid-1950s, my world in the Western Addition started at Octavia and Bush, where Morningstar School was located, and then west about four blocks to Buchanan Street, down to where the heart of Japantown was located. Usually, I'd leave school with a couple of friends and by the time we walked down Pine to Laguna Street, and turned the corner and walked down Bush Street, there's nine more guys behind us because the guys know that we're going to hang out and fool around, and there's going to be a bit more action than what mama wants you to do back home, which is usually going to Japanese language school!

I had a mixed group of friends. Japanese, Filipino, Black. Mixed, like the neighborhood. We had the J-town walk. The J-town feel. When we got down to the Fillmore, we'd check everyone out and they'd check us out, because you had to know who your rivals were. The Fillmore was tough, but happenin'.

Walking down Fillmore Street with my friends was so cool. There were movie theaters. Soul food restaurants. Pool halls. A bowling alley and a roller-skating rink. You walked by different doorways, and you started to hear doo-wop. In the middle of the afternoon, these guys are cutting it up, singing in the doorway because the marble floor gives a better sound.

You know how kids in the suburbs go to amusement parks, or some place like that where kids go there all day for amusement? Well, Fillmore Street was like that for me.

JOHN HANDY: I started playing music when I borrowed a saxophone from school. I borrowed it on Wednesday, and on Saturday I did my first gig at a rec center dance, and I've never stopped! I went to a high school in Oakland and there were kids in there that played music professionally. So I was learning a lot about music, playing with great players and sneaking over to Vout City and then Bop City when I was sixteen.

I later went to San Francisco State University and lived in the Western Addition on Lyon, between Fulton and McAllister, and later on Baker Street. A number of musicians lived right around me at that time. Jerome Richardson, the great multi-instrument reed player, lived across the street from me at one point. We rented from the same man, and we worked several gigs together. It was during my first year in college. On the next block was Eddie Walker, the trumpet player. He later married Sweetie Mitchell, the jazz singer. Eddie had a big house where a lot of musicians lived—some who later went on

John HANDY

Born in 1933 in Dallas, Texas, Handy moved to the Bay Area in 1948 and was soon playing his saxophone at various Fillmore nightclubs. After a stint in the U.S. Army, Handy moved to New York and joined bassist Charles Mingus's band. He returned to San Francisco in 1962 and has lived in the Bay Area ever since. Handy has recorded for many record labels and has earned Grammy nominations for both performance and composition. He had another taste of stardom with his funk-vocal crossover hit "Hard Work" in 1976. He lives in Oakland and continues to teach and perform internationally.

John Handy (left) in his early days of playing, 1950s. *Steve Jackson Jr.*

The Manor Plaza Hotel, 930 Fillmore Street, between McAllister and Fulton, mid-1950s. Many famous African American musicians would stay in the hotel while playing in San Francisco.

to make names for themselves: Teddy Edwards, a great saxophone player. Addison Farmer lived there, and his twin brother, who was a trumpet player. And a young guy, Sonny Clark, a piano player, moved in. So I got to know those people, and at one point we all were in a big band together, but just a few days before the first gig, I was drafted.

PAUL JACKSON: I went to Commerce High School with Vernon Alley. Living in the Fillmore I heard music all the time and I loved it. Sometimes Duke Ellington's band would stay at the rooming house near my house, which was owned by my neighbor. Black musicians had to stay in rooming houses and hotels in the neighborhood back then because they weren't welcome to stay downtown.

Paul JACKSON

Born in Alameda, California, in 1917, Paul lived in a foster home until the Jackson family adopted him in 1927 and moved him across the bay to the Fillmore. Surrounded by musicians in the neighborhood, he became a jazz fan and frequented many of the clubs.

Duke Ellington and friends in the Manor Plaza Hotel, circa 1950s. Musician Frank Jackson is peeking between the two standing women—one in a white flowered dress and the other in a dark flowered dress. *Steve Jackson Jr.*

Johnnie INGRAM

Coy about the exact date of his birth, Johnnie Ingram spent his childhood in Port Arthur, Texas. Ingram has been in music his entire life. At the age of eight, Ingram's piano-playing sister tried to teach him the instrument, but he wouldn't practice and stopped playing, a decision he regrets to this day. As a teen, Ingram began playing in local bands, first on banjo and then, when he joined Minor Brown's band, on violin. He decided to pick up the bass after seeing Cab Calloway's band at the age of seventeen, and he joined Milton Larkin's band in Houston with such well-known musicians as Ornette Cobb, Eddie "Cleanhead" Vincent, Fredrick Hayward,

and Illinois Jacquette. Ingram moved with his wife and daughters to the Fillmore in 1942 and was soon playing in all the clubs. Besides being a musician, he is a talented artist and photographer. He continues to play music regularly and lives in Daly City with his wife.

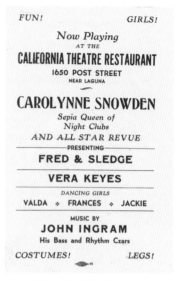

A flyer advertising the show at the California Theatre Restaurant, late 1940s.

JOHNNIE INGRAM: I came to California in 1942, and my wife and daughters came soon afterward. I thought there were more opportunities in California. We lived on the corner of Geary and Laguna. That's the only place people of color could live at that time. For quite a few years, they wouldn't rent to us in any other place, and sometimes not even in the Fillmore. Landlords would say, "We're filled up." But then a Caucasian person would go there and they suddenly had an opening for them.

It was the same thing with the unions. We couldn't get in most of the unions, and we were limited in the

Johnnie Ingram and his Rhythm Czars, late 1940s. *L-R*: James Sheldon, piano; Johnnie Ingram, bass;
Sammy Simpson, sax; Pat Everly, drums; Harold Phillips, trumpet.

Early 1950s promotional photo for Johnnie Ingram's band, Johnnie Ingram and his Rhythm Czars. *Designed by Ingram*

Johnnie Ingram and his Rhythm Czars playing at Jack's Tavern, late 1940s. *L–R:* Betty Allie; Willie James, sax; McKissic London Holmes, trumpet; Delmare Smith, drums; Johnnie Ingram, bass; Evelyn Myers.

jobs we could get. For example, when I first got to the Fillmore, I wanted to start a band, but I didn't know anybody. I had a family, so I had to get a job. I tried to get employed as an upholsterer, which is a job I knew how to do. So I went to an upholstery shop, and they said I had to join the union. So I go to the union, and they asked if I had a job. I said no, so they said, you get the job, and you come here, and we'll join you up, and the upholstery shop said, get in the union, and we'll give you a job. So I decided since I knew how to do all my own cutting and sewing, and they wouldn't let me in or hire me, I would open my own shop. It was the first colored upholstery shop in San Francisco, on Post Street near Laguna.

Mr. "Al" Franklin, new owner of the California Theater Restaurant, popular night club in San Francisco, is doing a fine job of making this club the nite spot of the city . . . Johnnie Ingram and his Rhythm Czars are giving out with some fine music and the crowds are starting back to this club . . . Mr. Roscoe "Cuby" of Omaha, Nebraska, is now the popular bartender on the day shift at this club, who has made many friends during the short period of time that he has been on the job.

Mr. Joe (Ivory) Hunter, the prince of the piano keyboard, and his (Three Star Trio), has moved to the Driftwood, an (O'Fay) spot located at 466 12th St., Oakland, with Miss Kathryn Gilbert on vocals and piano.

Late 1940s newspaper column discussing the California Theatre Restaurant and the Rhythm Czars.

Johnny Ingram and his Rhythm Czars went over to Treas. Isle the other day to entertain in the wards —and a stuffy Lt.-Comdr. refused to let them eat in the officers' dining room (where most entertainers get their chow). Despite the insult, they went ahead and did their stuff all afternoon for the hospital patients. The Red Cross is pretty hot about the whole thing. (Need I add that Ingram and his Czars are Negro?) . . . In answer to feverish pleas from the wolves, Jean Dean, the original Varga girl (and pal of Howard Hughes) is living at the Clift; take it from there . . . Incidentally, she'll appear here in July in "Mary Had a Little"—a title which might as well be changed right now to "Jean Has a Lot". . . The CIO-PAC will put the Bd. of Supervisors on the spot Mon. with a request for a resolution supporting continuance of OPA.

Herb Caen's May 3, 1946, newspaper column discussing the racism experienced by Johnnie and his band while entertaining ill soldiers at a Treasure Island hospital.

Bassists Johnnie Ingram and Eddie Hammon with Johnnie's artwork, 1998. *Lewis Watts*

Johnnie Ingram with an album of seventy-eight recordings of his bands, 1998. *Lewis Watts*

FRANK JACKSON: The Fillmore, when we came here, was open to everybody. Downtown, there were some problems. You were never told you couldn't go—you just got snubbed. You'd get an uncomfortable feeling. I could see what my parents had to go through in Texas. There wasn't any great big change when we moved here. It was just more subtle. You'd get "no" with a smile, instead of with a growl. I found that bitterness doesn't help you. You still have to live your life.

Frank JACKSON

Born in 1925 in Cleburne, Texas, Jackson moved to San Francisco's Fillmore District with his parents in 1942. Jackson knew he wanted to be a pianist and singer. He began playing in neighborhood clubs while still a teenager. Jackson and his wife, Kathy, live in San Francisco, where he continues to record and perform music.

The Frank Jackson Trio playing at Jack's Tavern, circa early 1950s.
L–R: Eric Miller, guitar; Charlie Oden, bass; Frank Jackson, piano.

L–R: Leo Amerdee, piano; a local singer; Teddy Edwards, and his girlfriend Angie at Bop City, circa mid-1950s.

Wesley Johnson Sr. with his Texas Playhouse barstaff. The dollar bills behind them were
later taken down to help pay for Wesley Johnson Jr.'s pharmacy school tuition.

WESLEY JOHNSON JR.: I actually remember when I was a little boy, with my brother and my mother, being turned down at a restaurant on the corner of Geary and Powell, which is right near Union Square in the heart of downtown San Francisco's shopping area. I didn't understand what was going on and asked my mom, "Why can't we eat here?" She was crying. "The man says he's not going to serve us." I asked her, "Why isn't he gonna serve us?" I didn't understand.

Later, in 1955, when I finished pharmacy school, I had a job interview at a pharmacy on the corner of Sutter and Powell. The person on the phone told me, "Bring your social security card. Come down now." When I got there, he told me to come not to his office but to the storeroom. He explained the facts of life to me—that it wasn't him, it was his customers. I just didn't buy it. I knew he was lying. So I could not get a job in San Francisco and almost took one in El Segundo [in Los Angeles County], but I said no. I borrowed some money from my father and opened a pharmacy on Sutter in the Fillmore.

Wesley Johnson Sr. being sworn in as school board member.
Wesley Jr. is seated beside his father at left.

Wesley JOHNSON JR.

Johnson was born in 1929 and raised in the Fillmore. His father ran his first nightclub, called The Subway, in North Beach. In 1942, Wesley Sr. bought a two-story building on Fillmore Street, remodeled it, and opened the Hotel Texas upstairs and his first Fillmore nightclub, the Texas Playhouse/Club Flamingo, in the storefront. He later started the Havana Club, another nightclub in the Fillmore, which enabled him to save enough money to put his son, Wesley Jr., through pharmacy school. Wesley Jr. later opened a popular pharmacy on Sutter Street, near Fillmore. Wesley Jr. passed away in 2004.

Wesley Johnson Sr. and T-Bone Walker inside the
Texas Playhouse, circa 1950s.

Wesley Johnson Sr. and one of the Club
Flamingo waitresses, mid-1940s.

WAYNE WALLACE: Although we moved from the Fillmore
when I was eight, we went back there often. My parents
liked to go to Wesley Johnson's Texas Playhouse, and
I studied music with a teacher on Sutter Street. Later,
I took lessons from Bishop Norman Williams, a well-
known musician who lived in the Fillmore. In those days,
musicians in the Fillmore were willing to help kids learn
to play music.

Music in the Fillmore was organic. In the air. It was
from the community and belonged to the community.
You can't look at the neighborhood without looking at the
music that was coming from the people who lived there.
Music also meant something to the people who ran the
clubs, not like today, where it is only about money. White
musicians like to come to the Fillmore because it was hip.
The Fillmore was a hot spot for music—a poor man's New
York City. It was exciting and even as a child, I always
wanted to know what was happening there.

FEDERICO CERVANTES: I did not live in the Fillmore, but I was getting introduced to the happenings there when I was in high school. The Fillmore had all of these little places, these little clubs, these eating joints or chicken houses. All had some sort of music going. They would have their doors and windows open and would be blaring the music out into the street.

The Melrose Record Shop was a really popular place. A lot of the records that I used to hear on radio stations KWBR and KSAN at that time could only be purchased at Melrose. You could get T-Bone Walker and Charles Brown. You could get a lot of people. I can't even name them all. That was the place to buy our records.

Wayne WALLACE

Wayne Wallace was born on May 29, 1952, and spent his first eight years in the Fillmore before moving to San Francisco's Ingleside District. He began his musical career on the piano, moving to the trombone in fifth grade. He credits his Balboa High School music teacher as an inspiring role model who got the budding musician to become serious about music. Wallace has recorded and performed with a variety of musicians, from John Lee Hooker and Chris Isaak to Sonny Rollins and Ray Charles. He remains a successful musician, recording and touring internationally while also teaching at universities around the country. Wallace still lives in San Francisco.

Federico CERVANTES

Soon after Cervantes's birth in 1936, his family moved from Virginia to Cuba, where he spent his childhood. He learned to play any instrument he could find, including the bugle, the trumpet, the clarinet, the violin, and what would became his signature—the piano. The family came to San Francisco while Cervantes was in high school. He soon discovered the wealth of music in the Fillmore. His first job in the neighborhood was at the Ellis Theater, playing piano for weekly talent shows. He then began appearing at all the local clubs, which led to his joining the Bop City house band. Cervantes's first recording was on World Pacific Records after his friend Chico Hamilton introduced him to the label's owner. He went on to record several albums and toured all over the world, but he would always return to the Bay Area. He passed away in 2004.

Wesley Johnson Sr. behind the bar of the Texas Playhouse, September 10, 1958. Although the Playhouse did not have live music, Wesley would often spin records and play DJ behind the bar.

SUGAR PIE DESANTO: We used to go to the Melrose and buy all our records. The Caucasian owner [jazz historian David Rosenbaum] was very, very nice to everybody. You were welcome. He sold everything. Jazz, blues, classical. It was a neighborhood store.

FRANK JACKSON: Maya Angelou worked at the Melrose. Marguerite Johnson, that's her original name. I remember her from my school days. We grew up together. She and I would sit on the porch and she'd read her poetry to me. I would sit there for hours sometimes and listen to the things she would write. And we would talk about things. She was always writing and reading. She left the neighborhood to get on with her books and poetry. We all know what happened to her!

EARL WATKINS: During the early 1940s, the Fillmore exploded, because the war industry started. Kaiser established his shipyards, and then you had all the different munitions plants on both sides of the bay. These industries started hiring Black people from the South, and naturally they came where we were. They all lived in the Western Addition. And that's when the Black business community in the Fillmore exploded. They brought their own restaurants, their own funeral services, their own nightclubs. People were war workers. They worked around the clock, so you had people on the street around the clock with money in their pockets and wanting to socialize. People would go out, the ladies would be dressed, and they'd ride public transportation. You had streetcars that went everywhere and all night.

ARMANDO P. RENDON: Once World War II was declared, the neighborhood changed. Overnight, the Japanese families that I had grown up with were gone. For a while, when they left, there was a quietness over the neighborhood that was unnerving. When the African Americans relocated to the Fillmore from the South, they began moving into the houses left behind by the Japanese and putting in businesses where Japanese-owned businesses once stood.

The Melrose Record Shop, 1226 Fillmore Street, 1947.
The advertisement on the window refers to a new blues single by Andrew Tibbs, "Bilbo Is Dead" [Aristocrat Records]. .
Theodore G. Bilbo was a Mississippi governor (and later senator) outspoken about his white supremacist views. *David Johnson*

Promotional photo for a Fillmore chorus line.
Several of the Fillmore nightclubs had chorus lines
during the 1940s and early 1950s. The photo is signed:
"To Mrs. Dorothy Hammond, from Nadine Cole."

STEVE NAKAJO: I often wonder what kind of community we, Japanese Americans, would have had here in the Western Addition if camp didn't happen. Japantown was changed forever because of camp. When the Japanese residents finally returned to San Francisco, four or five years later, it was really like starting over all over again.

EDDIE ALLEY: When the war started, a lot of people from all over came to San Francisco to work in the shipyards, and they ended up in the Fillmore. A lot of clubs formed in the Fillmore to entertain the new war workers. So I put together my own band consisting of Douglas Kinnard, Sam Allen, Sweetie Mitchell, myself, PeeWee Clayburg, Albert Claybrook, and Eddie Walker. We had new uniforms and were first-class. So we were always the first ones hired. Sometimes we'd be booked a year in advance. We were working every weekend. Regular nightclubs. Private parties. Later on, some of the white people heard about me, and they'd hire me to work downtown. Movie stars used to come out to the Fillmore District for the clubs. It was Harlem on a small scale. Harlem of the West.

A Japanese American wedding in the Fillmore.

R&B singer Ruth Brown with sax player Leo Wright on her right,
Booker T. Washington Cocktail Lounge, 1950s. *David Johnson*

L–R: John Handy, Pony Poindexter, John Coltrane, and Frank Fischer jamming at Bop City, circa 1950s. *Steve Jackson Jr.*

Sailors and their dates living it up, circa 1950s.

Crowd at the Texas Playhouse, September 10, 1958.

Pony Poindexter, saxophone; and Leo Wright, flute; on stage at Bop City, 1950s. *Steve Jackson Jr.*

A drummer in the Primalon Ballroom, late 1940s.
The nightclub booked only African American acts. *David Johnson*

L–R: Jimbo Edwards and Arthur Prysock at Bop City, early 1950s.

Al Smith jamming on drums with Pony Poindexter (center) and Teddy Edwards (right) at Bop City, 1950s. *Steve Jackson Jr.*

Women with hats at the Texas Playhouse, mid-1950s.

Murals decorate this unknown Fillmore bar, circa 1950s. *Steve Jackson Jr.*

Chapter 2

The NIGHTCLUBS

ALTHOUGH SAN FRANCISCO'S

AFRICAN AMERICAN POPULATION WAS RELATIVELY SMALL until World War II,

—

Fillmore Residents wouldn't dream of going to a bar or nightclub without dressing up. Texas Playhouse, late 1940s. *Steve Jackson Jr.*

the city still managed to make its mark in jazz history. While the Fillmore was one of San Francisco's main entertainment centers, from the early 1900s until the 1930s people of color were not welcome in the bars, nightclubs, and theaters that lined the streets. Instead, most African Americans went to the Barbary Coast, located on and around Pacific Street, adjacent to San Francisco's North Beach neighborhood. According to Tom Stoddard in his book *Jazz on the Barbary Coast,* the historical contributions of these jazz nightclubs, one of them co-owned by Jelly Roll Morton, should not be ignored.

Several major dance crazes that swept the nation were invented in the Barbary Coast, and, on March 6, 1913, the first printed use of the word *jazz* in connection with music appeared in an article about the neighborhood's clubs. But by Prohibition, most of the clubs had closed down, leaving a void for Bay Area musicians.

The 1933 opening of Jack's Tavern, also known as Jack's of Sutter due to its location on Sutter Street, marked the beginning of a new era in the history of African American music in the Bay Area. It was the first club in the Fillmore to be managed by and cater to African Americans. Soon after, the Club Alabam and the Town Club joined Jack's. By the start of World War II, with the explosion in African American population, dozens of additional clubs set up shop, including the New Orleans Swing Club, the Long Bar, the California Theater, Elsie's Breakfast Nook, the Texas Playhouse, and, later, the Champagne Supper Club, Leola King's Blue Mirror, and Bop City. Other, established dance halls such as the Primalon Ballroom and the Majestic Ballroom (renamed the Fillmore Auditorium in 1952) altered their bookings to include jazz, blues, R&B, and soul. The Fillmore scene began to be known worldwide, drawing Hollywood stars and famous musicians to the stages whenever they were in town.

Musicians playing in a Fillmore flat, 1940s. *Ricardo Alvarado*

EARL WATKINS: Before World War II, the main clubs that used colored musicians were in the Barbary Coast, which was near North Beach. There was a lot of employment for musicians in San Francisco until the authorities closed down the Barbary Coast in the 1920s. The musicians would come from the South, New Orleans, and parts of the Midwest. Sid LeProtti was one of the more well-known musicians from the South, and he also played in Los Angeles. In later years, someone wrote a book about Sid [*Jazz on the Barbary Coast*]. Many musicians worked days and played music at night. Fellows from here would go down to Los Angeles to do bit parts in the movies. If you see some of the older movies, you'll see the Black bands with musicians from San Francisco. But then the Barbary Coast closed down and the Fillmore took its place.

F. ALLEN SMITH: I had three weeks left in the navy and was stationed out in Pleasanton, where Santa Rita Prison is now. While there, I met some musicians from San Francisco who were mustering out: Vernon Alley, Earl Watkins, and Curtis Lowe. When they would take liberty I would go off with them to San Francisco, and they introduced me to the Fillmore. Vernon Alley was a big asset in turning me on to people in the neighborhood. Once I became a little more established, I moved to San Francisco—Geary Street between Octavia and Laguna. Of course that area has changed a tremendous amount from what it was in those days. There were two or three nightclubs on each block. It was just beauty to behold. I hate to say that the popularity of the area was due to the segregated situations in San Francisco at the time, but it was the case.

FRANK JACKSON: The first time I played for a live audience was in the Fillmore. I don't remember the name of the club, but it was on Fillmore Street, and the band leader was the saxophone player. He gave me my first real job, and I still wonder why because I didn't play very well! But I knew a lot of songs, and I could play well enough to get by on them. But the band leader liked me, and he taught me a lot of things, too.

Later I started playing with a lot of musicians, Earl Watkins, on occasion Vernon Alley, and Saunders King, to name a few. Saunders King sang and played guitar, and there were four other pieces in the band. I was the pianist, and once in a while I'd sing. King had a big hit in the late '40s, "SK Blues." I remember we did it, but I wasn't on the recording.

The Fillmore wasn't just Black music. Musicians here intermingled and worked together. They'd put a band together, and it had nothing to do with race, creed, or color. It had to do with how a musician played.

SUGAR PIE DESANTO: The Fillmore club scene was a mixture. You'd go in one club, maybe the Sportsman, and they'd be doing blues and jazz. You'd go down the street, and they'd be doing jazz. Then another place would be records. You could just go from one end of the neighborhood to the other, and every block had a club. If you were a musician and needed a gig, you just went to the Fillmore. You could make a living.

JIM MOORE: There were so many talented musicians that it wasn't a big deal if the organist Jimmy McGriff was at a club, because good music was so plentiful. Wherever you went, the standards were so high that you expected good music. Musicians knew exactly what they were doing, how to handle an audience. Otherwise the place wouldn't be packed. It was like watching the best painters, like Picasso, paint.

F. Allen SMITH

F. Allen Smith was born in August 11, 1925, and raised in Midland, a little steel town in Western Pennsylvania. Smith's mother, father, aunts, and uncles were all musicians. His uncle Clarence Smith was a minor celebrity as the trumpet player in Fats Waller's band. So it was natural that in fifth grade Allen picked up a trumpet lying around the house. He soon was playing with school bands and orchestras. His family relocated to Stockton, California, in 1943, and soon after Allen was inducted into the Navy, playing with many famous jazz musicians in the Navy Band. Once out of the Navy, he relocated to San Francisco, where he continues to live. Allen toured with many well-known musicians, among them Johnny Otis and Benny Goodman. He was also a popular educator who worked in the San Francisco school system for many decades.

Jim MOORE

Born in 1928 in St. Louis but raised in Memphis, Jim Moore and his family moved to Berkeley in 1940. A big music fan, Moore began visiting the Fillmore clubs in 1946. He later went on to start Sharp Records in 1969, which he changed to Jasman Records in 1970. The label's first recordings were of Johnny Talbort and Big Mama Thornton. Soon after, Moore began managing Sugar Pie DeSanto, whom he works with to this day. He currently lives in Oakland.

SUGAR PIE DESANTO: No bad stuff was tolerated. Oh no, honey! If they didn't like you, they'd send you off the stage. Everybody's hand would go up in the audience and you'd be waved off. That wave was something else. I've been fortunate enough that I've never been sent off the stage. Thank God it never happened to me!

JIM MOORE: People dressed. Entertainers dressed immaculate. Not like jeans and tennis shoes.

SUGAR PIE DESANTO: We came out full dressed. Suits and nice hats. Dressed to kill! You didn't go to the clubs during those days looking hoochie coochie. Hats, minks, whatever—everybody dressed up.

JIM MOORE: People would come from church and go to the clubs. But they weren't dressed up because they were coming from church. In those days, Black people had a culture. There was more cohesiveness, and there was more tradition and pride. We all had jobs and were doing pretty good for that era.

SUGAR PIE DESANTO: You'd have all kinds of races. Everybody partied. It wasn't about the color.

A well-dressed crowd at an unknown Fillmore nightclub, circa 1950s. Dr. Carleton Goodlett, editor of the *Sun-Reporter*, is in the middle in a light colored suit. *Steve Jackson Jr.*

Placard for Jack's Tavern, late 1940s.

Flyer for New Jack's Lounge, mid-1970s, featuring
Houston Person and Etta Jones. This was one
of several locations Jack's moved to after the closing
of the original Sutter Street location.

JACK'S TAVERN/ JACK'S OF SUTTER 1931 SUTTER STREET

Although dances were held and bands played at Fillmore venues
such as the Majestic Ballroom and the Bal Masque Ballroom, people
of color were not welcome at most of the clubs until the beginning
of World War II. One of the first nightclubs to cater specifically to
African Americans was Jack's Tavern, also known as Jack's of Sutter,
which opened in early 1933 and was first owned by Lenna Morrell
and later passed through several hands. The club featured the hot
jazz sounds of local musical favorites, such as the Saunders King
Band. Later, many famous musicians, including Charles Mingus,
played there. It was also the first club to establish the Fillmore as
a jazz district.

Robert Lee (left) at Jack's Tavern, 1950s. Robert Lee was known as "the player of the players" and, according to several Fillmore musicians, could procure anything one might need.

EARL WATKINS: Jack's Tavern was on Sutter between Fillmore and Webster, and soon after, around the corner the Club Alabam opened up. The Club Alabam was run by Lester Mapp, who had been involved in running some of the Barbary Coast clubs. Later, there was a club that opened practically next door to Jack's called the Town Club, so in that early period, before the war, we had the big three.

In those days, Jack's was a very nice club, considered more of an elite establishment, and the Club Alabam was smaller and a little more down-to-earth. I started going to Jack's around 1939 to see Saunders King with his small group. About that same time, Herb Caen, who later went on to become a well-known newspaper columnist, came to San Francisco to start his journalism career. Vernon Alley had gone to college in Sacramento with him, and when he came to town as a reporter, naturally he looked Vernon up. Vernon was starting to make his musical mark. He played at the Club Alabam with Wilber Beranco, one of our excellent pianists, and Bob Barfield, who was the saxophone player of note. Vernon took Herb around to the colored clubs, and Herb plugged Jack's and the Alabam. So they ended up with a mixed clientele and put the Fillmore District on the map.

PAUL JACKSON: The first bar I went to was Jack's of Sutter. I was around fifteen. My father found out I was in there and came in and jerked me off the bar stool. He wasn't too happy. Jack's was owned by Mr. Love, an African American man who lived upstairs in a flat above the bar. You went through a single front door, and the bar was on

Robert Lee with the bartender at Jack's Tavern, also
known as Jack's of Sutter, 1950s.

An ad for Jack's Tavern from the 1944
San Francisco phone book.

one side, and there were three booths on the other side of
the room. In the back was the dining room and the bandstand, which was in the middle. You could get dinner
there from 7 P.M. until 2 A.M. Saunders King and his band
played there a lot.

JOHNNIE INGRAM: Jack's Tavern was the first place I played
in the Fillmore—1943. Jack's always had good music,
and because of this it was packed, with a line outside the
building to get in. They served good food and had tables
with nice tablecloths; small, but first-class. People dressed
up, with fancy hats, nice dresses, and furs. Men had to
have a necktie, suit, or a sport coat, or you wouldn't get
in the door.

My five-piece band alternated with Saunders King's
band—his band would play a week, and then my band
would play a week. On the off-weeks, we'd play other
places. It was ironic that I was alternating weeks with
Saunders, because when I first got to San Francisco,
Eddie Taylor, the fine tenor player, tried to get me to join
Saunder's band, but I didn't want to because I wanted
my own band. Jack's did so well that if the club closed for
a few weeks so that the owners could take a break, my
whole band got paid, and we got a vacation.

FRANK JACKSON: Jack's had two crowds. During the day
and early evening they served food, so they had that
crowd, and then the night crowd were jazz enthusiasts.
It was a good scene, a mixed crowd, and people used
to dress up. In the '50s Jack's also had variety shows,
accompanied by the house band—singers, dancing girls,
comedians. I worked there with Redd Foxx and Slappy
White for a while. They did their routines six nights a
week for a couple of months.

Inside Jack's Tavern, 1931 Sutter Street, 1950s.

The **CLUB ALABAM** 1820a POST STREET

In 1935, Lester Mapp, former manager of Purcell's, one of the most popular Barbary Coast nightclubs, and Louie Varette, a local music aficionado, opened the Club Alabam, just a few blocks from Jack's. According to Tom Stoddard in *Jazz on the Barbary Coast,* Mapp was a West Indian from Barbados who came to San Francisco as a sailor on a boat and never left. The heavyset man "with a powerful wallop in each hand" ran several clubs in the Barbary Coast and in Oakland before opening his club in the Fillmore. The Club Alabam closed in 1946 and was known as the Club Iroquois in 1947. Charles Sullivan, a local African American businessman who later became the largest promoter of African American music west of the Mississippi, took over the space in 1948 and renamed it the Club Sullivan. In 1950 it again became known as the Club Alabam before closing for good in 1953. Lester Mapp died in 1951.

L-R: Frank Jackson, piano; Walter Sanford, bass; Junius Simmons, guitar, 1950s.

EDDIE ALLEY: In the early '30s, the only clubs in the Fillmore were the speakeasies. That's where I began playing. I was really young. Then the Club Alabam opened up. It was a big club but not lavish, with people sitting down at tables, listening to the music. I was part of a little band that played there, led by Mike Lysinger.

EARL WATKINS: Club Alabam was owned by Lester Mapp, Louie Varette, and another guy whose name I can't remember. Vernon Alley, a bass player, Wilbert Baranco, on piano, and Bob Barfield, a saxophonist, were the original trio who played at the Alabam. In fact, Vernon and Bob were playing there when Lionel Hampton, who was playing over at the 1939 World's Fair on Treasure Island, came to the Alabam and jammed with them. Lionel was so impressed that he asked Bob and Vernon to be in his band, and when Lionel left town, they went with him. Wilbert stayed in San Francisco and became a popular music teacher.

FRANK JACKSON: In the 1940s I would work at the Alabam, but it didn't pay too much, so if you had a chance to play another gig, you'd work somewhere else. On the weekends it would do pretty well, but during the week you could shoot a cannon through there! You'd go see somebody at the Alabam and there would be four or five people in that big room.

Helen Simmons, wife of bass player Junius Simmons, dressed for a night on the town, late 1940s. In the 1940s and '50s, the scene at the Fillmore bars and clubs inspired patrons to don their finest attire.

The TOWN CLUB
1963 SUTTER STREET

The third jazz club to open, in 1936, was the Town Club. It was located just a few buildings down from Jack's Tavern but was much smaller and more low-key than either Jack's or the Club Alabam. A local businessman named Jim Robinson ran the club. It closed sometime in the mid-1950s.

EARL WATKINS: I never played the Town Club, but I remember going by it when I was a teenager. It was a small place, smaller than most of the other clubs, with a few tables and a piano. Ed Hammond on bass and Pat Patterson on piano made up the house band. They would have jam sessions in there on Sundays.

The outside of Minnie's Can-Do Club, early 1970s.
Jimmy Salcido

MINNIE'S
CAN-DO 1915
FILLMORE STREET

In 1940 a fourth club joined the Fillmore jazz scene, setting up shop in a former radio store named Pickett's. Minnie's Can-Do was the Fillmore's longest continuously running jazz club in the same location, but it finally had to move in 1974 to 1725 Haight Street before closing for good in the late 1970s. The Victorian building that housed Minnie's survived redevelopment and is now occupied by a popular upscale restaurant.

EARL WATKINS: The first club I played was a place on Fillmore, between Bush and Pine, next to a little alleyway, called Minnie's Can-Do. As it happened, a fellow named Jimmy Brown, a bass player who had been taking lessons with Vernon Alley, formed a band and he needed a drummer. At that time, I was so inexperienced, I had been practically just beating on pots and pans! So I got a small drum set at a pawn shop, joined the union, and was in the band. That was 1940. Pat Patterson was the piano player, and I was playing drums, and Jimmy was on bass. We were playing after hours for $2 a night at Minnie's Can-Do. They were bootlegging, too.

Advertisement for Louis Armstrong at the
New Orleans Swing Club. Owner Louis Landry
is pictured in the upper right star.

Advertisement for a fashion show at the New Orleans Swing
Club, 1950. Local clothing stores would put on several fashion
shows each year to highlight the latest fashions.

NEW ORLEANS
SWING CLUB 1849 POST STREET

According to musician John Coppola, Louis Landry opened the New Orleans Swing Club in the early 1940s. Originally from New Orleans, Landry came to San Francisco to work in the shipyards in Richmond. After noticing that thousands of Louisiana transplants had no place to buy New Orleans food, he quit his job at the shipyard and ran a successful business selling down-home cooking to the homesick shipyard workers. Landry, who had always wanted to be a promoter, took his money and invested it by opening the nightclub. It closed in the early 1950s and became the Champagne Supper Club.

EARL WATKINS: Louis Landry decided he wanted to open up a nightclub. So he took a vacant lot and built a club himself. He had that kind of skill! He called it the New Orleans Swing Club, because he was from New Orleans. He began booking bands—big names like Kid Ory—in there. There was a period when he even had Louis Armstrong and his band.

Neighborhood clothing stores often put on shows, such as this Fillmore Fashion Show, at local nightclubs.

Fillmore Fashion Show, with music, 1950s.

John and Frances Lynne COPPOLA

John, a trumpet player, and Frances, a singer, played and sang in many of the Fillmore clubs. John was born in 1929 in New York but grew up in Oakland, alongside Johnny Otis. John wanted to be a clarinet player, but when his mother went down to the music store to buy her son the instrument, the trumpets were on sale, so she bought one, and he became a trumpet player. Once he began to play professionally, John became a member of several house bands at different Fillmore Clubs, including the New Orleans Swing Club. He also played with Henry Mancini, Woody Herman, and Frank Kenton, among others. Frances Lynne, as she goes by professionally, was born in 1926 in Dallas, Texas, and moved to California at the age of twenty, in 1946. She gained fame as the vocalist for Dave Brubeck's band during the 1950s and 1960s, and she went on to sing with both Gene Krupa and Charlie Barnet. The couple still lives in San Francisco, where they continue to teach and perform.

JOHN COPPOLA: The New Orleans Swing Club, also known as the New Orleans Swing House, was owned by Louis Landry, a gentleman from New Orleans. Like many, he came to California to work in the shipyards in Richmond, but he lived in the Fillmore. He quickly saw that there was no New Orleans-style food available, but there were hundreds of folks from Louisiana pouring into the neighborhood. So he got some food wagons, served up real New Orleans food, and made a fortune.

Landry always wanted to become a promoter, so when he made money, he opened up the Swing Club. He wanted it to be like New York's Cotton Club, filled with stars, and, for a brief time, it was. Louis Armstrong played there, with Jack Teagarden and Earl Hines. Basie

Dexter Gordon jamming at Bop City, 1950s. *Steve Jackson Jr.*

Dave Brubeck Quartet with Francis Lynne (Coppola) sitting in front of the piano, 1949. Francis sang with Brubeck for several years.

Billy Shuart Band, 1950. *At the mic:* Shuart, leader and vocalist. *Front:* Jack Spiers, Jack Shore, Paul Desmond, Chuck Travis, Earl Davis, Bob Lowry, Andy Anderson. *Back:* Lenny Tigart, Wyat Reuther, Bab Hotaling, F. Allen Smith, John Coppola, Al Del Simone.

played at the club with Buddy DeFranco for one week. Saunders King and Jerome Richardson played there. Nick Esposito, the guitar player, also played there.

I was a member of the house band. One night, I think it was January 1950, I showed up for work as usual, and the place had been padlocked by the IRS. No explanation, nothing. I found out later that apparently Landry had been fixing the books and stashing the extra money under the bandstand. He went to jail, and Curtis Mosby, who had been a band leader on the East Coast and manager of the Club Alabam in Los Angeles, moved up to San Francisco and took over the New Orleans Swing Club. He changed the name to the Champagne Supper Club.

ALLEN SMITH: One night I saw Dexter Gordon leaving the New Orleans Swing Club, walking across the street toward a bank to get into a car. I thought he was the most handsome man in the world. And dressed! His clothes were so tailored and beautiful. He had an incredible topcoat on. But at the same time, it wasn't a big deal. You'd see famous people all dressed up walking around the Fillmore all the time. I saw Duke Ellington in the Fillmore. Miles Davis in the Fillmore. Dizzy Gillespie was in the Fillmore. You name them, they were there. It was a big party, and you never slept. We were young and anxious! One of the best times of my life.

CHAMPAGNE SUPPER CLUB 1849 POST STREET

In 1952 Curtis Mosby came up from Los Angeles and, with Don Barksdale, took over the space formerly occupied by the New Orleans Swing Club. They renamed it the Champagne Supper Club, keeping the upscale image established by the Swing Club. The Champagne Supper Club remained open until 1957.

FEDERICO CERVANTES: By yesterday's standards, the Champagne Supper Club was kind of a nice, fancy place, especially for African Americans at that time. Not just a place off the street where you would walk in and would have to duck right away because someone was throwing a bottle. I would go there underage. I was scared to death, but I wanted to be on stage, and eventually I finally did get a chance to play. Vernon Alley played there with his group, also Curtis Lowe and Sammy Simpson.

FRANK JACKSON: The first place Billie Holiday sang in the Fillmore was the Champagne Supper Club. It was probably the mid to late 1950s. She also appeared at a downtown club called the Say When, on Bush. I was in their house band at the time, so I got to hear her every night. She was pretty sick by then, so they would help her up on the stage, and she'd sit on a stool, and sing like she was twenty years old! Boy, it was amazing. She was there for two months, and it was a real treat to hear her. She stayed in the Fillmore. She and Leola King, owner of the Blue Mirror Nightclub, were very good friends. They were big buddies.

EARL WATKINS: In 1955 Jerome Richardson and I got a gig playing four nights a week at the Champagne Supper Club. The second week I showed up to play, and Jerome was gone. He had left with Father Hines and went to Los Angeles, and from there he drove to New York. But prior to that, Jerome was with Lionel Hampton's orchestra

A typical crowd in front of the popular Champagne Supper Club,
1849 Post Street, 1950s. *Steve Jackson Jr.*

during the same time Quincy Jones was with him. Quincy was just a kid, a teenager. So when Jerome went back to New York, he reconnected with Quincy Jones, and he went over in the early '60s to Europe with him. When they got back to New York, Jerome was doing studio in New York, and Quincy came out to California and started working in Hollywood. Later, Jerome came to Hollywood and worked on *The Carol Burnett Show* and also with Quincy Jones for years. Eventually he ended up back in New York, and he passed away in New York. Jerome was an excellent studio player. He went to San Francisco State. He was there at the same time with Rudy Salbinini, Paul Desmond, all those guys. They all used to sit in at Jack's and the Alabam after school.

Dancing at a Fillmore nightclub, late 1940s. *David Johnson*

Billie Holiday and Mel Tormé (right), 1950. *Steve Jackson Jr.*

ELSIE'S BREAKFAST NOOK/HAROLD BLACKSHEAR'S CAFÉ SOCIETY 1739 FILLMORE STREET

Elsie's Breakfast Nook opened soon after World War II in the basement of the Temple Theater building, a rundown movie theater. The club only lasted a few years before it was bought by prize-fighter Harold Blackshear and several unknown investors in late 1946. Changing the name to Café Society, Blackshear remodeled the space, taking it more upscale. Unfortunately, the club only lasted a few years, closing in 1949. The entire building was later demolished by the Redevelopment Agency in the 1960s.

EARL WATKINS: In the '40s, up there across from the Havana Club and up close to Sutter Street, was Elsie's Breakfast Nook. It was down in a basement, underneath a store and theater. Elsie was one of the first club owners in the Fillmore to go after-hours. And that place, man, it would be packed. That was around 1946, 1947. And one night I went in there, and who should be in there? Robert Mitchum! Then Elsie left it, and Harold Blackshear, the prizefighter, took it over, and it became a café. He called it the Café Society.

Tuli ALSTON

Tuli Alston grew up in the Fillmore and lived across the street from Jack's of Sutter in the 1930s and 1940s. Because of his proximity to the Fillmore jazz clubs, he became friends with many of the musicians and would often be on the scene. Tuli still lives in San Francisco.

EDDIE ALLEY: Blackshear's was a nice club, a high society club for Black people. Right nice, and people dressed nice and everything. Joe Lewis came there one time with his two girlfriends. He was something else. He wouldn't talk to the girlfriends. He didn't have to!

BOBBIE WEBB: One Saturday night, when I was on Fillmore Street, selling my papers, I saw Billie Holiday go into Blackshear's, a club underneath the Temple Theater. It was a very nice little club, down some stairs with carpet on the floor and nice decorations. I couldn't believe Billie Holiday was going in there.

ALLEN SMITH: I had a little five-piece group at Harold Blackshear's, and one week we played opposite Billie Holiday. She came through San Francisco and played there with a small group. Couldn't have been more than a rhythm section and herself. It must have been the late 1940s or early 1950s.

FRANCES LYNNE COPPOLA: When I first came out to San Francisco, I found out about the Fillmore neighborhood and began to go there to listen to music. Harold Blackshear's was my favorite nightclub. They had great bands and sometimes I'd sit in with whatever band was on the stage and sing.

TULI ALSTON: Elsie's was in the basement of the Temple Theater. It was an after-hours joint that featured music, much like Bop City was later on. Elsie's began the whole after-hours club tradition in the Fillmore. Benny Carter played there, Vivian Danders played there, Vernon Alley and Earl Watkins played there. In the late 1940s Harold Blackshear, one of the first Black prizefighters to win a title, took it over and changed the name to Café Society. His backers thought that Harold's name would draw people to the club, but it didn't last too long, though, and closed sometime in the 1950s.

JACKSON'S NOOK 1638 BUCHANAN STREET

Mr. and Mrs. Jackson opened this restaurant and impromptu nightclub in 1940. They sold it in 1950, and the new owner changed the name to Jackson's Theater Restaurant. It closed in the mid-1960s.

ARMANDO P. RENDON: Mr. and Mrs. Jackson were light-skinned African Americans. Creoles. Their grandson Herman lived with them. I knew him from school, and sometimes we'd go over to his grandparents' club. The Nook was a restaurant in the front, with a large room and in a somewhat large backroom. They were open all night, and when Bop City was crowded, musicians would go over to Jackson's Nook to play in the backroom, and patrons would follow them. It was a nice place to be. No illegal dealings, just fun. And the Creole food was good, too!

FRANK JACKSON: After being onstage for a while at Bop City, sometimes I'd get off and go over to Jackson's Nook. It was on Buchanan Street, right around the corner from Bop City. It was a restaurant, and they had an old upright piano in the back room. Guys used to go there when Bop City got crowded and have a jam session.

ALLEN SMITH: All the musicians would meet at Jackson's Nook for breakfast or lunch, because it was so close to Bop City. There was always a little jamming going on there. The musicians couldn't resist playing.

The
LONG
BAR 1633
FILLMORE STREET

Fillmore Street between Geary and Post Streets, 1952.
Note the Long Bar on the right.

According to Fillmore legend, the Long Bar had the longest bar in the world. Storefront-turned-nightclub in the mid-1940s, the Long Bar featured many big names in jazz. It closed in the late 1950s.

PAUL JACKSON: The Long Bar was one of the bigger clubs. It was a storefront, and you would walk in off Fillmore Street, but the bar went all the way back to Steiner Street, which was the next block.

FRANK JACKSON: The Long Bar was one of the longest bars I've ever seen! I played at the Long Bar with Slim Gaillard. He did comic stuff and some commercial things and was a very good entertainer. Strange man, too. One night, all of us in the band showed up except for Slim. At 8:45, about fifteen minutes before we were supposed to start, Slim called the club and told the owner he was in San Jose, but he said he was on his way. We were a four-piece band, and he was the fifth, so the band could function without him. The club owner, a huge guy named Carlette who had a nice personality, kept asking us when he was coming. We kept saying, "He's on his way."

I think Slim got there about eleven o'clock. When he arrived, he brought the cab driver with him and told the club owner to pay him, which he did! Slim spoke to a few people and then went back in the kitchen and baked a cake, sliced it, and came out and served everybody cake! He never played that night, and nobody said a word about it, not even the owner!

ARMANDO P. RENDON: For a time, the piano player Erroll Garner appeared at the Long Bar on a long-term engagement. One night I was out front, looking in from the door because I was underaged, watching Erroll play. He went on a break, and someone from the audience got up and began to play the piano in his place, copying Erroll to a tee. Erroll became very irate and insisted that the man be thrown out. It was really funny, but I don't think Erroll thought so!

Earl Grant on piano, Junius Simmons on guitar, circa 1950s. Junius was born and raised in the Fillmore and later became a minister.

The outside of the Club Flamingo, September 26, 1944.

The TEXAS PLAYHOUSE/ CLUB 1836 FILLMORE STREET FLAMINGO

The first bar venture of Wesley Johnson Sr.'s was the Subway Club in North Beach. Once the Fillmore took off as a jazz hotspot, he sold his part of the Subway and opened up a small hotel with a bar in the street-level space on Fillmore Street. The bar was known as both the Club Flamingo and the Texas Playhouse. It closed in the early 1960s, and the building was taken over by the San Francisco Redevelopment Agency. It remained vacant until the early 1970s, when Jack's of Sutter was briefly relocated into the space because its former location was torn down to make way for an apartment complex. The Playhouse's building suffered the same fate in 1975.

WESLEY JOHNSON JR.: It was 1942, and the war was on. My father already was a partner in The Subway, a club in North Beach, when he decided to buy a building on Fillmore Street and remodel it. It was a two-storefront building with flats upstairs. The bar, which he first called the Flamingo and later the Texas Playhouse, was downstairs, and he converted the flats into a thirteen- to fifteen-room hotel that he called the Exclusive Hotel

Bar patrons outside the Club Flamingo, mid-1940s, with the awning
for the Exclusive Hotel Texas visible behind.

Waiter pouring drink at the Club Flamingo, December 17, 1944.
Owner Wesley Johnson Sr. remodeled the bar in
the early 1950s and renamed it the Texas Playhouse.

Texas. My grandmother and father came to San Francisco in 1915 from Beaumont, Texas. A reporter wrote about the hotel opening and said, "What's so exclusive about a hotel for Negros?"

My father spent his last money before he opened the Flamingo to buy twelve suits. He explained to me that nobody likes to do business with somebody who looks poor. He felt that having a good time was worth more than money. Over the years, my father remodeled the place several times. For the second remodel, he had $3,500 in silver dollars embedded in the bar. He commissioned John O'Shanna to create some murals. He's the same artist who designed the Fisherman's Wharf logo.

These murals were in bas-relief and gold and silver leaf and featured well-known musicians of the era.

There was no live music. My dad played records. He was the entertainment. But most musicians came by as customers because that's where their fans were. They liked it because they wouldn't be required to perform.

DOROTHY ALLEY: I worked there as a waitress when Wesley first opened. Wesley knew me when I was born, my whole life, so he gave me a job. It was kind of fun. It's too bad Wesley Johnson wasn't an entertainer, because he loved to entertain everybody who came in. He'd play records in the back and dance up and down the bar. It was pretty nice, and Wesley kept things under control. You walked in there, and if you even looked funny, you were out! He didn't stand for any foolishness.

Wesley Johnson Sr., in white cowboy hat, with bartender Zeke Thomas inside the Texas Playhouse, 1950s. The bar was embedded with silver dollars that were later pulled up, according to Wesley Johnson Jr., to pay for his pharmacist's degree.

Pat Regina Johnstone, circa 1950s.
Signature reads: "There's no man like a Texas man, He gets things done! Love to Wesley. Hi! There "Tex," I love you! Pat."

SUGAR PIE DESANTO: I used to go to a lot of clubs—the Morocco, the Sportsman, the Playpen on Divisadero. And I used to go to the Texas Playhouse. I was young, but I'd build myself up with tennis balls or whatever. A couple of times I borrowed my brother's socks and then tied a pillow on the back of my go-go to make myself look big and wore a lot of makeup. I got in easy. Except that some of the club owners really looked and said, "Are you sure?" My feet didn't even reach the bottom of the bar chair! I'd say, "Yeah, I'm old enough. Give me a scotch and soda!"

One time my father came into the Playhouse and caught me. He pulled me by my ears and got me out of there. He told me, "I don't want you to shake your, you know." He took me home by my ear. I was so embarrassed.

FRANK JACKSON: The Playhouse was popular, and most of the time you couldn't get in. It was beautiful—elegant, but small. Ladies came in free, and the guys had to pay and were required to wear a jacket and tie. If you came in and didn't have a tie, Wesley had ties there for you. He demanded respect for the ladies, and got it, or you had to go. There were often crowds standing outside. One afternoon I stood there talking to Louis Armstrong. He was outside smoking, taking a break from working downtown.

BOBBIE WEBB: As a youngster, I sold the *Sun-Reporter* newspaper around the Fillmore. I picked up my papers on Thursday after school, and I would go into every hotel,

Emile Clifton, a.k.a. Konjo Koiff the Mad-Gician, 1950s.
Clifton was a Medal of Honor Tuskegee Airman.
Signed: "To Texas Boy Johnson from Magic-Man Clifton."

Lionel Hampton and Scottie, last name unknown, 1950s. Signature reads:
"To Mr. Wesley Johnson from Hamp and Scottie." The walls of the Club
Flamingo/Texas Playhouse were covered with photos given to owner Wesley
Johnson Sr. Some of the photos later ended up being given to Red Powell and
were hung inside his shoe-shine parlor.

Bar patrons in front of Zeke Thomas/Wesley Johnson painting inside the Texas Playhouse, circa 1950s.
The murals were created by John O'Shanna, who also designed the Fisherman's Wharf logo.

Patrons of the Texas Playhouse, early 1950s.

Wesley Johnson Sr. (second from left)
and the bartenders of Club Flamingo, mid-1940s.

Stationery from the Club Flamingo/
Texas Playhouse, late 1940s.

Birthday party at an unknown Fillmore nightclub, 1950s. *Steve Jackson Jr.*

Bobbie Webb on air at KPOO Radio,
San Francisco, 2005.

bar, restaurant, and beauty parlor in the neighborhood to sell my papers. I had to sell them all by Sunday, so every Saturday night I would go to the Texas Playhouse, because it always had a crowd. At some point I had told the owner, Wesley Johnson, that I was from Texas. Well, he liked anyone who was from Texas, so when I came in through the door, Wesley would grab me, stand me up on the bar, and would yell out to everyone, "I want everyone in the club to buy a paper from my boy from Texas!" So every Saturday night I would sell out all my papers because of Wesley! (laughs) Later, when I became a man and married, I moved right next door to Wesley. He lived at 3045 California and I lived at 3055 California. I really liked him, and got to know his two sons. He was a good man.

Bobbie WEBB

Saxophonist Bobbie Webb born in 1945 in Tyler, Texas. The youngest of four children, Bobbie and his siblings were raised by their grandmother, who moved them to San Francisco in 1945. The family found a home in the heart of the Western Addition, at Sutter and Baker. Bobbie began playing his horn in his early teens, getting his training in the Fillmore clubs. Bobbie continues to make his mark as a blues saxophonist, KPOO (89.5 FM) disc jockey, and founder and director of the Blues and R&B Music Foundation. He still lives in the Fillmore.

Billie Holiday and Wesley Johnson Sr., with her beloved dog,
at the Club Flamingo, circa early 1950s.

Mural from the walls of the Club Flamingo highlighting well-known musicians from Texas, November 8, 1945. Saunders King (far right) was a popular San Francisco musician who had a minor hit in the late 1940s with the song "SK Blues."

Curved bar of the Club Flamingo with Jacques mural against the back wall, mid-1940s.

Wesley Johnson Sr. and customer at the Texas Playhouse, 1950s.

Group at the bar of the Club Flamingo /
Texas Playhouse, circa World War II.

REMEMBRANCE

By Antoinette Brossard

Due to the passing of time, many patrons in the photographs taken inside the Fillmore nightclubs remain unidentified. Several years ago, Lewis was contacted by someone who recognized a couple sitting at a table inside the Club Flamingo/Texas Playhouse. The photograph was being displayed as part of a history panel on Fillmore Street. Antoinette Broussard, niece of Robert Broussard, tells their story below.

Robert Willard Broussard and his longtime sweetheart, Carrie Bell Patisaw, spent many evenings enjoying what they loved, the nightclub scene in San Francisco. As his niece, I remember how impressive Uncle Bob looked dressed up in East Coast style, prepared for the evening drive to San Francisco where he picked up Carrie Bell in his nice car, with the destination of the Fillmore jazz clubs ever paramount in his mind.

Born in McCloud, California, to parents John and Eugenia Broussard, who migrated from the South during the Jim Crow days, Bob spent his childhood growing up in Stockton, California. He loved horses and dreamed of becoming a jockey. As a youth he would sneak out to the Stockton racetrack, sometimes working as an exercise rider for the racehorses.

Later he settled with his family in Oakland, California. As an adult, he rode with the Black Cowboy's Association, and he rode his beloved horse, Dream, in Oakland's annual cowboy parade. He also liked to bet at the racetrack, where he became a good handicapper.

In 1942, during World War II, Bob joined the navy. He lost a lot of his boot camp buddies in the Port Chicago explosion, when they were assigned to ships to handle ammunition but had no prior training or experience. After leaving the navy in 1946, Bob moved to the East Coast. As a jazz lover he told stories to his nieces and nephews about living in New York City, hanging out in the Cotton Club, and meeting many talented musicians, among them Duke Ellington and Count Basie.

Bob returned to California in 1950 and worked at the Naval Air Station in Alameda, retiring in the late 1980s having worked forty years as an aviation structural mechanic. There he developed a love for airplanes and spent time satisfying his flying hours.

Carrie Bell died long before Bob on January 31, 1971. This photo is proof of their bond, and I imagine how much he must have missed her when she departed. Her name was the name you always heard connected to Bob's. He used to take her kids out as he did his nieces

and nephews. As a child he took me to see the San Francisco Ballet productions, and afterward sometimes we visited Carrie Bell and her family, a home filled with warm smiles and joy.

After he retired, Bob kept busy working as a part-time bartender and security guard. Whether he lived on the East Coast or West Coast, you could find him on either side of the bar, pouring drinks and making friends. Since the Fillmore clubs had closed down he spent time off frequenting the Oakland clubs he loved, including The End Zone, Bozen's Locker, and Sweet Jimmy's.

Bob always had a great smile, great jokes, and kindheartedness. Never married, he lived with and provided support for his sister, Simonetta, and mother, Eugenia, as they in turn appreciated and loved him. His humor provided family and friends the answer to a frequently asked question about his everlasting bachelor status. Bob said with a smile, "Why get married? I can be miserable by myself!" Bob died at eighty years old on December 30, 2002, four days before his sister Simonetta died from a long illness, on January 3, 2003. We believe he came back to get her just in time for both of them to catch the tail end of the New Year's festivities in the spirit world.

Robert Willard Brossard and sweetheart, Carrie Bell Patsaw, mid-1950s.

Club Flamingo/Texas Playhouse owner Wesley Johnson Sr. kisses Leola King's hand, September 10, 1958. *Wesley Johnson Jr. Collection*

Leola KING

Leola King was born in 1919 in Los Angeles, California. Her father moved north to San Francisco in 1943 and began a successful and popular barbecue restaurant business. Leola joined him in 1946, and she opened her own business—nightclub and bar—in the early 1950s. She added several other bars to her stable of businesses before redevelopment wiped them out. Leola continues to live in the Fillmore.

The BLUE MIRROR 935 FILLMORE STREET

In 1940 the Gold Mirror Cocktail Lounge took over a restaurant called the Minnow Buffet and converted the space into a bar. Some accounts note people of color were not welcome, while others state that the club had a mixed clientele. Everyone agrees that the bar did not do very well until Leola King, daughter of a popular barbecue restaurant owner, took over the space in 1953. She began booking mainly blues and R&B bands, and the club quickly became packed nearly every night.

Leola King at the Club Flamingo/Texas Playhouse, September 10, 1958.

LEOLA KING: I was born in 1919 and grew up in Los Angeles. I was a dancer, singer, and actress down there. My father came to San Francisco in 1943 and opened up a barbecue restaurant in Oakland. It did so well that he rented an empty lot on Geary Street near Laguna, right across from where the Sequoia Apartments are now, from Charles Sullivan. Dad bought a log cabin from Horsetrader Ed, the car dealer, which was sitting on his car lot, and moved it to the empty lot on Geary, then started a second barbecue restaurant. It was extremely popular and made a lot of money. Lines out the door. I moved up to San Francisco in 1946 to help him out. I decided to open my own place in the early 1950s and took over a nightclub called The Gold Mirror, which I changed to The Blue Mirror. I had the club until 1970, when Redevelopment closed it down.

PHILIP ALLEY: The Blue Mirror was a nice club, owned by a friend of my father and mother's, Leola King. She was a heck of a woman. Tough, but a beauty. She was the type of woman who knew how to handle people. She could talk to the pimps and hustlers. She didn't play around, and they knew how to conduct themselves in her club. She had a good mix of musicians at her club, local people and musicians that came through. I saw Earl Grant there. Jimmy Smith. Big Bill Patton.

FEDERICO CERVANTES: The Blue Mirror was on the sophisti-cated side, not saloonish. It and the Champagne Supper Club gave a little more prestige to the Fillmore. The Blue Mirror was owned by Leola King. She was strictly business from what I could see. Dollars and cents. Fast talking, show me what you can do. That sort of thing.

Earl Grant played the Blue Mirror. I attended some of his performances. At the time, what he was doing was unique to the scene. The African American approach to music was either deep into rhythm and blues or deep into bebop. Not sitting and singing standards like Earl did. But he had a following, and after he started recording, the following grew. Leola was very happy with him.

JOHN GODDARD: I was always a collector of stuff, and when I got into music, I went from Elvis Presley to Little Richard to Muddy Waters in the space of about six months. I had parents who were nuts enough to let me start going to concerts when I was thirteen. To this day, I still don't understand why. I used to hop on a bus and go to the Fillmore Auditorium, the San Jose Civic, and other venues around the Bay Area by myself. The first show I saw was Bobby Bland and Junior Parker. I saw Ray Charles, Lloyd Price, the Platters, James Brown. A little white kid with a Brownie camera, stealing posters off the phone poles outside and up near the front, taking pictures and getting autographs afterward.

I mainly did auditoriums, but I would go over to Fillmore Street and just stand outside the nightclubs,

A fourteen-year-old John Goddard with Sugar Pie DeSanto at
the Veterans Hall in Redwood City, 1958.

John GODDARD

Born in 1943 in Mill Valley, California,
John Goddard became interested in music
when he was thirteen. As a teen, he traveled
around the Bay Area to see his favorite
acts. At the same time, he began working at
Village Music, a record store in Mill Valley,
later buying the business and turning it into
an internationally known destination for
collectors of music and musical memorabilia.
John still lives and works in Mill Valley.

listening to the music from the street because I wasn't old enough to go in. I remember being outside the Blue Mirror and seeing T-Bone Walker. He played there regularly. So did Jimmy McCracklin. Lowell Fulson. I wouldn't say it was crowded, but it was busy. Good club. Back then, being on Fillmore Street was like being on Basin Street in New Orleans at three in the morning. It was a real busy scene. I'm sure there were people doing stuff they shouldn't have been doing, but I felt safe. Never once got hassled. Not once. I never considered that maybe it wasn't a good idea for me to be there.

SUGAR PIE DESANTO: The Blue Mirror—now that's one place I remember. I sang there with T-Bone [Walker]. He was a regular. It was a real small place, and they'd hire entertainers. Blues. Lots of blues. If you wanted to hear the blues, you went down to the Blue Mirror. It was unusual for a woman to own a club, but Leola King stood her ground. You didn't mess with Leola. I don't think so!

FRANK JACKSON: I first met Leola because she worked for her family. They had King's Barbecue on Geary and Buchanan. Then I worked for Leola King at the Blue Mirror. It was a nice club, and she was great to work with. We became good friends. I worked there with my own trio and with T-Bone Walker. He was fun to play with. Lots of guitar. That man had the Midas touch. He could play and he had fire. T-Bone's son was also working with us then. He played guitar just like his dad, so his dad must have taught him.

BOBBIE WEBB: I began to go into the nightclubs when I was sixteen. We all had fake IDs that said we were twenty-one, so we could go into any club or bar in the Fillmore, and that's where I really learned to play. During that time, the late 1950s and 1960s, the Fillmore area was not about jazz, it was about blues and R&B. We had more rhythm and blues clubs than we had jazz clubs, and the bigger jazz places were in the Tenderloin and North Beach.

One of my favorite places was the Blue Mirror—Leola King's joint. You'd walk in and there was a bar on one side, with about fifteen tables behind it and a stage in the back. Not a very big place. But as small as that place was, Leola was able to bring in top-named bands. I played the Blue Mirror with T-Bone Walker, the Ink Spots, and Little Willie John. Leola knew everyone, so she was able to get the best bands of the day into her club. Because of this, the place was always full.

Leola King's Blue Mirror, 935 Fillmore Street, in 1966. Although the nightclub was small, Leola was able to book top-name acts due to her friendships with many of the musicians.

Neighborhood children try out Louis Jordan's instruments, early 1950s.

ELLIS THEATER

1671 ELLIS STREET

The Ellis Theater, originally known as the Princess Theater, was built as a burlesque and vaudeville hall in the early 1920s. In 1942 it became a movie theater and was named the Ellis. In the early 1950s, with movie attendance falling, the theater owners added a talent night. Attendance increased dramatically, and people from all over San Francisco flocked to try and win the weekly $50 prize. The theater closed in the 1960s due to redevelopment.

FEDERICO CERVANTES: In the '50s, there were several places in the Fillmore that had talent shows. One of the most popular was the Ellis Theater, on Fillmore and Ellis. A radio personality named Fatso Perry ran the show, and as his name indicates, he was quite obese. I got on the musical map from getting a little prize—$50, big money at that time. After that, I was hired as the accompanist for the program, playing the piano behind other people. The Ellis was usually crowded. A lot of people dropped in because it was a chance to play music, and their friends came to hear them. They would dress up for it. It was a happening.

One time Billie Holiday was in town, and it was rumored that she was supposed to drop into the Ellis. And one night she did. I couldn't appreciate all of her glory because at the time the name Billie Holiday didn't mean much to me, except for the fact that everyone that night was screaming "Billie Holiday!" They asked her to sing a song, but she wouldn't do it.

SUGAR PIE DESANTO: All us kids used to go every week to the Ellis. It was a movie theater, and they would show the old cowboy movies. Then around 8 P.M., they'd have a spot for a talent show. I said, "Well, shoot, if they can do it, I'm gonna try my hand!" They had a little band, and they'd ask what key you'd want, and then you'd go ahead. Each time I went, I would win $25 and two lamps! I got mad one time because the DJ, Rockin' Lucky, didn't want to give me my lamps. I almost tore the back of the theater up. I was really upset.

Johnny Otis would come by the Ellis occasionally to pick up talent. One night, he was in the audience, and after I won, he came up and asked who I was. He said I had a different voice—heavy. Today, there are very few that carry that kind of heavy. Maybe Gladys Knight or Etta James. We're of the old school. Everybody's gone up

in the clouds to sing. But we got that belt. Real heavy in the basement.

Johnny said, "Well, you're kind of young." I said, "Yes, I know!" Then he asked me if I would like to record, and I told him—I'll never forget it—"Are you crazy? A record?" He scared me to death. Then he explained that he felt I was talented and asked me to come to Los Angeles. That did it. He discovered me there, took me to Los Angeles, and recorded my first record. I was fourteen. Ever since then, I never shut up! My father didn't think too well of it, but my mother let me go. She hid it from my father. He didn't discover it until later on, when I was sixteen or seventeen.

We were in the recording studio when I got my name. My real name is Polaya Ballington Davis, but Johnny said, "You can't go around with a name like that!" He said, "What name do you want?" I had no idea because I was young. I was real short, so short that when they put me in front of the mike at the recording studio, they had me stand on two Coke boxes and maybe a telephone book or two to reach the mike. He looked at me and he said, "You look like a little sugar pie!" And that did it. I recorded the record, returned to the Fillmore, and started doing the clubs. In 1959 I had my first hit. I haven't stopped since.

Guitar player at the Primalon Ballroom, I950s. *David Johnson*

The **PRIMALON BALLROOM** 1223 F̲ILLMORE STREET

This cavernous Fillmore hall went through many incarnations in its lifetime. In the 1930s it was used as miniature golf links. In 1934 it became the Woodland Dancing Hall. Then, in 1945, the name was changed to the Brown Bomber Café, and the place was turned into a German beer garden and roller-skating rink. In 1949 the name was changed to the Primalon Ballroom. The ballroom was used for multiple purposes until it closed in 1961. The building was demolished in 1974.

EARL WATKINS: The Primalon Ballroom was also called the Brown Bomber. Before World War II, it was a German beer garden. Then in the interim period the Young Communist League took it over, and it was like a recreation center and a social center. When it was a beer garden, it was segregated. When the Young Communist League took it over, they welcomed us, and we'd go there as teenagers. They had a pool table and just social activity. Later on, I saw Dizzy Gillespie play there.

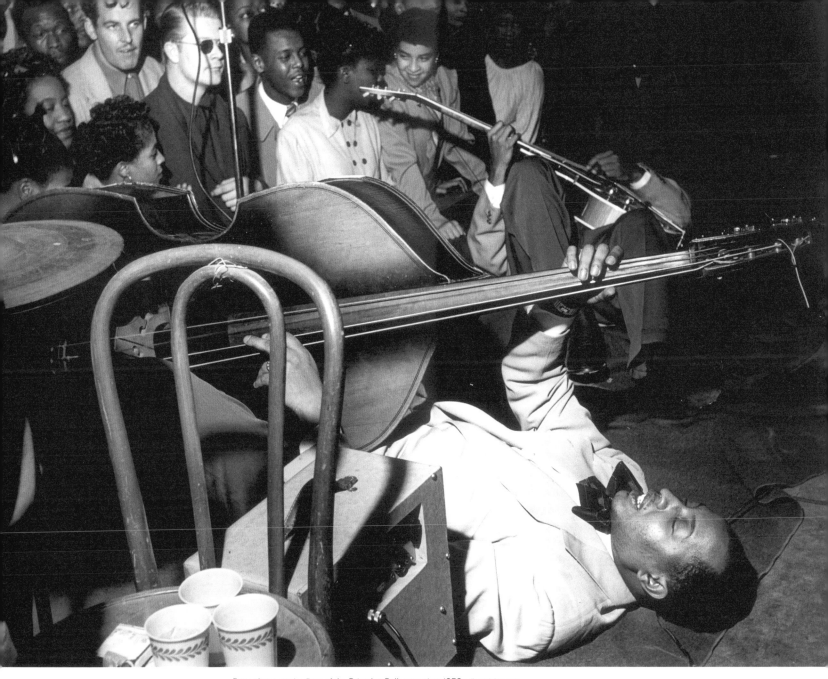

Bass player on the floor of the Primalon Ballroom, circa 1950s. *David Johnson*

Mixed crowd at the Primalon Ballroom, 1950s. The ballroom featured music on the weekends, and during the week the tables and chairs were removed and the venue turned into a roller-skating rink. *David Johnson*

James and Carrie McCoy, owners
of the Primalon Ballroom and
the Manor Plaza Hotel, circa 1950s.

Women inside the Primalon Ballroom, 1950s. The wallpaper behind
the women was designed by LaWanna Taylor's mother, Carrie McCoy.

LaWanna TAYLOR

LAWANNA TAYLOR: After my parents married, they saved
up their money and began to buy old Victorian houses in
the Fillmore. They renovated the properties and rented
them as rooming houses. They later got into the nightclub
business, and it was my mother who named the club the
Primalon Ballroom. She was a very creative woman. My
parents originally operated the business as a roller-skating
rink, and then began promoting music. During the week-
days, the Primalon operated as a roller-skating rink, and
on the weekend, when they could book the bands, it was
operated as a nightclub. My parents were Black and they
promoted Black blues bands, and consequently, the major-
ity of their patrons were also Black.

I was three years old when my parents opened the
Primalon. They had special roller skates made for me and

LaWanna Taylor grew up at 1350 Golden Gate
and Fillmore, just three blocks from the Primalon
Ballroom nightclub run by her parents, James
and Carrie McCoy. James McCoy was born in Seattle,
Washington, while Carrie was born in Long Switch,
Mississippi. The couple met in the Fillmore in the
1930s, and they had LaWanna in 1946. Carrie and
five of her six children, including LaWanna, moved
to Colfax, California, in the early 1960s. LaWanna
still lives in the Sierra foothills town.

A nearly all-women band performing at the Primalon Ballroom, 1950s.
Women musicians were rare during this era.

The interior of the Primalon Ballroom as it was set up for music, 1950s. During the week, the tables and chairs were removed, and the ballroom turned into a roller-skating rink. Note the padding on the columns.

The lounge area of the Primalon Ballroom, 1950s.

a little outfit. They joked that I learned to walk and skate at the same time! I remember the building as being very large. Hanging on the outside was a neon sign showing a girl roller-skating, which flashed on and off. Coming to the entrance, you would walk up the stairs to a landing where the ticket window was located. There was a small room where Mama would sell tickets, and where we could stay while she worked, and Daddy handled what was going on in the ballroom. Before the doors opened we could go upstairs and watch the performers rehearse, returning downstairs before showtime. As the guests began to arrive, we could peek out and see all the ladies and gentlemen in their fine evening attire. We could hear the music and feel the vibrations of the people dancing above. I can remember lying there and watching the neon

girl skating sometimes to the beat of the musicians before I fell asleep.

To promote the bands, my parents would have window cards printed and they would put my brothers and me in the back seat of Daddy's Buick Roadmaster and drive around the Bay Area posting them in businesses and on telephone poles.

The Fillmore District, in the early 1950s where the Primalon was located, and where I grew up, was multicultural. White, Black, Chinese, Greek, and Mexican families, all lived and worked there, and I do not recall any serious problem with racism. I remember it as being a thriving neighborhood.

In the late 1950s my parents bought a 100-room hotel located on Fillmore and McAllister. My mother

The basement of the Manor Plaza Hotel, used for music in the 1950s.

Inside the lobby of the Manor Plaza Hotel, 1956.
James McCoy is on the far right.

named it the Manor Plaza. Her original idea was to make it a rooming house; however my father's idea was to operate it as first-class hotel with a bar, restaurant, barbershop, and nightclub in the basement, so that is what they did. In fact, Flip Wilson worked as a bellman for them. I believe that may have been part of the reason the Primalon was closed. Since they were "hands-on" business operators, they probably became overextended. My older brother, Jim, says he remembers that the roller skates were left in the vacant building and that kids would break in and steal the skates.

FRANK JACKSON: The Primalon was fun. I went there when it was a roller-skating rink, and they had big mirror balls. I was a lousy skater! Later, a lot of times they would have famous big bands—Lionel Hampton, Basie—and then they'd have smaller combos, too. Man, it was great. I was always hanging around the bandstand.

JOHN HANDY: I played at the Primalon several times, once with PeeWee Crayton, and once with the singer Ernie Andrews. Leo Wright, the alto player, and I would back them up. It was mainly a blues place, with a blues crowd. Mainly Black, but a few whites came in. Someone told me it had been a roller-skating rink, which doesn't surprise me, because it was pretty big. Actually, the sound was quite good. We didn't have the kind of sophisticated equipment we now have today, but yeah, you could hear the band, and that's all I cared about!

L–R: Drummer Bobby Osborne and sax and flute player Leo Wright, early 1950s.

Billie Holiday backstage, 1958. *Jerry Stoll*

The Ambassador Roller Skating Rink, later the Fillmore Auditorium, mid-1940s. The steel arches and lights were torn down during World War II for scrap metal for the war effort.

The FILLMORE AUDITORIUM
1805 GEARY BLVD

Few night clubs in the world are as famous as the Fillmore Auditorium. Built in 1912 by three women who were land-poor, the Majestic Hall & Academy of Dancing quickly became a popular place of entertainment. The name was changed in 1928 to the Majestic Ballroom and again, in 1936, to the Ambassador Dance Hall. From 1939 until 1952, the hall was turned into a roller-skating rink. Charles Jordan Himes began holding dances there in 1949, and Charles Sullivan took over booking bands in 1954 and renamed the club the Fillmore Auditorium. On December 10, 1965, a new era was ushered in when Charles Sullivan allowed Bill Graham to use his dance-hall permit to host a benefit for the San Francisco Mime Troupe. The event was such a success that Graham began booking performers at the auditorium when Sullivan did not have shows. In November 1966, Sullivan was found murdered in San Francisco's South of Market neighborhood. Graham took over booking the club until the popularity of the music forced him to find a larger space on Market and Van Ness, which he renamed the Fillmore West. The Flamin' Groovies, a local band, took over booking the club for a brief time in the late 1960s until 1971, when it became a Black Muslim Temple. In the early 1980s, promoter Paul Rat renamed the venue The Elite Club and hosted dozens of punk rock shows. In 1986, a Berkeley promoter named Michael Bailey took over the club and began holding concerts under the name the New Fillmore Auditorium. Graham, wishing to return to the venue where he got his start, took over the auditorium from Bailey in 1988 but kept him on as the booking agent. Graham passed away in 1991, but the Fillmore continues on as one of San Francisco's most popular concert venues.

EDDIE ALLEY: In the 1930s I played at the Fillmore with Wesley Peoples and his band. The hall was owned by some Jewish people, and it had an all-white audience. We were the first Black band that ever played there, but people of color were not allowed in the audience. I played there later, in the '50s, when Charles Sullivan ran it.

VERNON ALLEY: I remember the Fillmore Auditorium well. In the 1930s big bands would play there, like the Dick Jergins Band and the Saunders King big band. Wesley Peoples, my brother, and I were part of the house band. But the problem was that the dance-hall owners would not allow minorities in to see bands, or to roller-skate when it was a rink, until Charles Sullivan took it over in the '50s and began booking bands again.

SUGAR PIE DESANTO: Charles Sullivan had the lease on the Fillmore Auditorium. He used to book me. He did all the bookings for big names, entertainers like James Brown and Gladys Knight. He was into the big productions. If you wanted to get a big gig, you better call Charles or you wouldn't get one. He was an honest man, but just don't cross him. I played there in the '50s. I wasn't hot yet with a record, but I wheedled my way in to do a couple of gigs. Then I returned with James Brown after I had a hit record.

JIM MOORE: Charles was a nice guy, the nicest promoter I ever met. Gentleman. Strictly a gentleman. He was the largest promoter of African American music. He'd start bands on tours in Seattle, Sacramento, Oakland, San Francisco, Stockton, and four or five gigs in L.A. He was

CHARLIE SULLIVAN Our 'Mayor' is still offering you the best in bottled sp. irits and his fast delivery service can't be beat. Give us a ring he say as we are as far from you as your te. lephone. LIL ALLEN is currently knock. ing em' out at the New Orleans Swing Club. We like her very much and I am sure you will say the same after hear. ing her rattle the 88's.

Newsletter blurb about concert promoter Charles Sullivan, known as the "mayor of Fillmore Street," 1950.

Handbill for 1920s dance at the Majestic Ballroom. The ballroom was segregated until 1952.

Beginning in 1940, the Fillmore Auditorium space was used as a roller-skating rink, known first as the Ambassador Roller Rink, later the Majestic Roller Rink. The rink, which did not admit people of color, was closed by new owner Harry Shifs in 1952 because noise from the skates could be heard in the shops below. He reinstated music in the hall, which was known for the first time as the Fillmore Auditorium.

In 1954, Charles Sullivan leased the Fillmore Auditorium and began promoting concerts. He became the largest promoter of African American music west of the Mississippi. In late 1965, Sullivan allowed Bill Graham to borrow his dance hall license, launching Graham's career. Sullivan was murdered in late 1966. These posters announce two of Sullivan's early 1960s concerts. Jimi Hendrix was the guitarist in Little Richard's band.

Poster for the Ike & Tina Turner Review, booked by Charles Sullivan at the Fillmore Auditorium. Jimi Hendrix, known as Jimmy James at the time, played in the band during this tour.

the man. He was the circuit. You never worried about getting paid. Sometimes he would pay the guys ahead of time. Say, if you were going to Seattle to accompany someone, he'd pay you here.

JOHN GODDARD: I started going to shows at the Fillmore Auditorium in the late 1950s. It was a little funkier than later when Bill Graham had it, but it wasn't that much different. The Fillmore at that time wasn't really mixed. Ninety-five percent of the audience was Black. I never had any problem. Every once in a while someone would come up to me and say, "I'll keep my eye out for you, and if anyone gives you any trouble . . . " Because I was just this little kid. I can see where I might have had problems if I was with half a dozen guys, but I always went by myself.

A lot of the big names, like Bobby Bland, had reviews with their own emcees that came through the Fillmore.

People like James Brown and Ike and Tina Turner would travel with half a dozen of their own acts, and they'd just do this review—four or five singers, and then it's star time. They didn't have local bands that opened for them.

My favorite Fillmore show was Little Richard. The auditorium was packed, but then again, I never went to the Fillmore during that era when it wasn't packed. Charles Sullivan really brought in the big-name acts. I was a huge Little Richard fan, and I was up front, taking tons of pictures. It was only years later that I found out that the guitar player, who kept getting in the way, was Jimi Hendrix. I remember him because he played with his teeth and behind his neck, but to me that night, he was just this guitar player who kept getting in the way of me taking pictures of Little Richard.

Little Richard and guitarist Jimi Hendrix onstage at the Fillmore Auditorium, October 1964, captured by a teenage John Goddard on his Brownie camera.

Crowd at the Plantation Club,
1628 Post Street, 1950s. *Steve Jackson Jr.*

The PLANTATION CLUB 1628 POST STREET

Originally, the Plantation Club was a Japanese restaurant owned by K. Kurskige and opened on December 29, 1914. It is unclear how long the space remained a restaurant, but it was taken over by Peggy and Leslie Armstrong in 1946. The club stayed open until 1961, when it became the Korea House restaurant. Although the Redevelopment Agency requested to demolish the building in 1975, it appears to have survived, as an older building stands on the lot to this day.

JOHN HANDY: I don't remember playing the Fillmore Auditorium until the '60s, but I did go see Dizzy Gillespie there in 1956. He was with a big band. I believe that was the first time I was there. In the early '60s, during the Civil Rights Movement, I played there with my group called the Freedom Band, and as a member of CORE, the Congress of Racial Equality. I helped organize the concert.

EARL WATKINS: In 1946, Peggy and Leslie Armstrong opened up the Plantation Club. It was a supper club where Wilbur Hobes played, as did Henry Red Allen and his orchestra.

FRANK JACKSON: The Plantation was in two rooms. They had a bar and a piano downstairs, and from time to time they would have a cocktail piano, and I played there. Upstairs, they also had a bar and a dining room. For a long time, they did shows up there, too. The owner, Les, introduced me to Willie Mays. He hung out at the Plantation.

EDDIE ALLEY: The Plantation was very, very nice. Robert Mitchum would come in and sing with the band once in a while, and other movie stars would come there.

L–R: Ella Fitzgerald, Robert Lee, Don Newcomb, football Hall of Famer Joe Perry, and others in front of the Booker T. Washington Hotel, 1950s.

The
BOOKER T. WASHINGTON HOTEL & COCKTAIL LOUNGE 1540 Ellis Street

Rebecca Weinberg opened the six-story, 115-room hotel in 1910 as a rooming house. It was known as the Hotel Edison until the early 1950s, when it was renamed the Booker T. Washington Hotel. In the lobby was a cocktail lounge, booked by Charles Sullivan until his death in 1966. Among the noteworthy musicians were Stuff Smith, the jazz violinist, and Bobbie Webb. The hotel was also a popular place to stay for traveling musicians. Count Basie, Billie Holiday, and Dinah Washington with her two children and a tutor all stayed there. Slim Gaillard took over the kitchen and would cook for jazz musicians. The hotel was closed and torn down in 1970.

FRANK JACKSON: I worked with my own combo at the Booker T. I lived about a block away, so all I had to do was walk across the intersection and go to work. The pay wasn't all that great, but aside from there being a lot of work, you got a lot of experience. And you got to meet a lot of people you wouldn't have.

JOHN HANDY: My very first jam session I ever attended as a musician was at the Booker T. Washington Hotel Lounge. They had jam sessions in there every night. I had come over from Oakland with some older musicians I knew and got me on stage. There was a great tenor player from Amos Milburn's band named Willie Smith sitting in, and Stanley Willis and Kermit Scott also played. That was the first time I ever played in the Fillmore.

JOHNNY OTIS: I used to come up to the Fillmore from Los Angeles, looking for talent. I found a lot of musicians and singers that way. It was fertile ground. Before I discovered Sugar Pie DeSanto, I discovered her cousin, Etta James, or, rather, she discovered me. Etta came up to the hotel in the Fillmore where I was staying. She was sixteen, arrogant, yet shy. She just barged into my room, turned toward the bathroom, and started singing at the tile for better acoustics. I was impressed and offered her a singing job on the spot. She said she had to call her mom, so I handed her the phone. She had a conversation, told me her mom said yes, and she came

OLLIE MARIE ADAMS BLUES & TORCH SINGER

RECORDING EXCLUSIVELY FOR
PEACOCK RECORDS INC.
4104 LYONS AVENUE
HOUSTON, TEXAS

Ollie Marie Adams, 1950s. She sang with Johnny Otis and his band.

Johnny OTIS

Born in 1928 in Vallejo, California, Otis began playing at Bay Area clubs in 1939. He moved to Los Angeles in 1943 but would return to the Fillmore to find talent for his band and record label. He discovered Etta James and Sugar Pie DeSanto in the Fillmore. Otis continues to play with his band and hosts a weekly radio show syndicated on Pacifica Radio. He lives in Sebastopol, California.

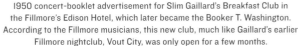

1950 concert-booklet advertisement for Slim Gaillard's Breakfast Club in the Fillmore's Edison Hotel, which later became the Booker T. Washington. According to the Fillmore musicians, this new club, much like Gaillard's earlier Fillmore nightclub, Vout City, was only open for a few months.

Unknown photographer sitting in the lobby of the Booker T. Washington Hotel, 1950s. The Booker T. was one of two popular hotels where African American performers stayed while playing in San Francisco.

with my band that night to Los Angeles. I later found out there was no one on the phone, and her mother didn't know where she was for a few days!

BOBBIE WEBB: The Booker T. was a great big tall white hotel, fifteen or sixteen stories high. All of the major Black entertainers lived at the Booker T. when they were in town. It was the place to stay and be seen. As a young newspaper seller, the first place I'd head over to after picking up my papers would be the Booker T. because there were always so many people there. I'd walk up and I would see these great big shiny buses in front of the hotel. Bobbie Blue Bland's bus. Duke Ellington's bus. I couldn't believe those buses. Parked out in front of that hotel, all shiny.

Ironically, my blues band, Bobbie Webb and Company, ended up being the very last band to play at the Booker T. Washington Hotel's lounge before they tore the hotel down. It was 1970, a Sunday evening and a nice night. I'll never forget it. It was crowded, but we always had a crowd on Sunday evening. The Booker T. had a bar and lounge on the first floor, and people would come down from the rooms upstairs to enjoy the entertainment, plus the public could walk in. It wasn't very big—could only seat about fifty people at the most. We played a great gig that night, and the very next day they began demolishing the hotel. It was so sad, because it wasn't falling apart. I guess it was just in the way. A little paint and it could have lasted for thirty or forty more years at least.

The Ella Commings Dancettes, 1950s. Several of the Fillmore clubs, such as the California Theatre Club, featured shows with a chorus line.

The CALIFORNIA THEATRE CLUB RESTAURANT 1650 POST STREET

The Cherryland Sukiyaki Restaurant was a neighborhood Japanese supper club until 1942, when Japanese Americans were forced into relocation camps and Cherryland closed. A Hawaiian African American named Julius Delifus and several partners took over the abandoned space, renamed it the California Theatre Club Restaurant, and began featuring elaborate entertainment, including a chorus line of dancing girls and famous musicians and bands. It closed in 1947 and became the Gourmet Theater Restaurant until 1953, when Mrs. Kaey Mizogani took it over and returned the space to a Japanese eating establishment called the Tokyo Parlor Restaurant. The restaurant closed in 1961, and the building was demolished.

A 1944 San Francisco phone book ad for
the California Theatre Restaurant.

EARL WATKINS: The California Theatre Club was across the
street from Charles Sullivan's liquor store. It had been
called Cherryland before the war, and the Japanese ran it.
When the Japanese went to the camp, Julius Delifus, the
fellow that had the Havana, and a fellow named Fleming
went into partnership, took over Cherryland, and turned
it into the California Theatre Club Restaurant. It was
first-class, with food, dancing, and a floor show. They
brought acts from back East. George Dewey Washington,
a very fine singer from the old-time vaudeville days, was
a mainstay there. In '46, through mid-'47, maybe up into
early '48, I played there with Johnny Cooper and Curtis
Lowe as the house band. I'll never forget when Paul
Robeson showed up one night and sang on stage. Lee
Young [Lester's brother] and his band also played there.

Exotic dancer Velva Velvet at the California
Theatre Restaurant, 1946.

JOHNNIE INGRAM: The California Theatre Restaurant was just like a Hollywood club. In fact, acts and reviews from Hollywood clubs would come up to perform. They had nightly shows. The waitresses were all in uniform, and you couldn't have found a better place if you had gone to New York. My band played there, Jake Porter's band out of Los Angeles played there, Jack McVea also came up from L.A. and played there. The California Theatre Restaurant was *the* place, at the time.

FRANK JACKSON: I never played there, but I saw Saunders King perform, and a pianist named Cedric Haywood had a band there. Jerome Richardson was there as well.

Julius Jacquet, sax; Bill Hathaway, piano; Walter Oakes, bass at the Havana Club, early 1950s.

The HAVANA CLUB 1718 FILLMORE STREET

The building that housed the Havana was one of the older buildings in the neighborhood. The earliest reference to it was in February 1907 as a cigar store and saloon owned by Albert Herbert. In 1926 a restaurant was added. It became the Havana Tavern in 1934 and was taken over by Julius Delifus in 1942. In 1950 it was called the Havana Club. Wesley Johnson Sr. bought the three-story building in the late 1950s and kept it open until the early 1960s, when Redevelopment took over the building before demolishing it in 1969.

WESLEY JOHNSON JR.: Julius Delifus, who came to San Francisco from Honolulu, bought the Havana Tavern in the '40s. It was a bar that occasionally had music. Cal Tjader played there with Walter Oaks, Pat Patterson, and Bill Hathaway.

EARL WATKINS: The Havana was a small club—narrow—but it was packed.

WESLEY JOHNSON JR.: In 1954 my father bought the club and changed the name to the Combo. It stayed open only a few years after that.

The exterior of Bop City, mid-1950s. *Steve Jackson Jr.*

VOUT CITY/ BOP CITY 1690 POST STREET

One of the most famous Fillmore Clubs, Bop City, on Post Street at Buchanan, got its start in 1949 as Vout City. The club was run by the handsome and colorful musician Slim Gaillard, who had a good ear for music but a lousy business sense. The club quickly folded, leaving Charles Sullivan, a prominent African American business-man, to find a new tenant. Sullivan approached Jimbo Edwards, who was working as a car salesman at the time, about the space, and in 1950 Edwards agreed to open up a café, calling it Jimbo's Waffle

Shop. When local musicians discovered an unused back room and began holding after-hours jams, Bop City was born. The club quickly became a magnet for every famous and not so famous jazz musician visiting San Francisco. Bop City closed in 1965, and the wooden Victorian that housed the famous club was moved around the corner to 1712 Fillmore Street. It now houses Marcus Books, a store dedicated to African American reading and educational material.

Jimbo Edwards with the infamous "signed" Bop City bass, which musicians described as the worst bass in the world. *Jerry Stoll*

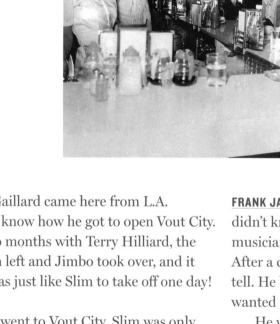

An early portrait of Jimbo Edwards, taken soon after he opened Jimbo's Waffle Shop, early 1950s.

Left: Interior of Jimbo's Waffle Shop, 1950s. Louis the cook was known for his fried chicken.

FRANK JACKSON: Slim Gaillard came here from L.A. Business-wise, I don't know how he got to open Vout City. I worked there for two months with Terry Hilliard, the bass player. Then Slim left and Jimbo took over, and it became Bop City. It was just like Slim to take off one day!

JOHN HANDY: I actually went to Vout City. Slim was only there a short while. It wasn't as well developed as Bop City later became. It was just basically a room with a few tables and chairs, and they had table service so that you could order. But really, it was bare bones.

EDDIE ALLEY: Slim Gaillard was one of the most fantastic performers I ever knew in my life. He was a brilliant guy, but a nut in one way, an eccentric.

FRANK JACKSON: When Jimbo first opened the club, he didn't know anything about jazz. He used to ask the musicians, "Is that person good, or is that one good?" After a couple of years, his ear got sharp and he could tell. He learned, because he was very interested. And he wanted good musicians.

He would let anybody come in, and they'd get a chance. If they weren't making it, he would get them off the stand quietly and tell them to go home, practice for a while, and come back when they were ready. He'd do it nicely. He had to do that sometimes because some of those kids would go buy a horn and two weeks later they were trying to play, and that didn't work too well.

Besides music, Jimbo had special dinners. Louis was his cook, and he had fried chicken and chicken in the

An early 1950s jam session at Jimbo's Bop City, before the club became internationally known.

basket for $5. I'm telling you, his chicken was really something else! Most of the time he'd run out of chicken quick.

ALLEN SMITH: Jimbo was a sweetheart person. Everybody I know liked Jimbo. Nobody had a bad word to say about him. Very quickly, Bop City became *the* after-hours spot.

JOHN HANDY: Bop City was like a second home. Musically, for me, it was my first home. It was probably 1949 when I started going there. At times I was part of the house band. Bop City was not just a club; it was more than just that. So much more.

FRANK JACKSON: There were quite a few after-hours spots in the Fillmore, but Bop City was the most famous. It was really a workshop for musicians, a place for learning. You got a chance to play with the good, the bad, and the ugly! Musicians would sit around and talk to each other about musical things, about chords and putting things together, and how they execute and how they finger things. You were surrounded by all of that.

JOHN HANDY: One night, I came over to the Fillmore from Oakland with some older musicians who had just graduated from my high school. One of them, Skippy Warren, a talented local bass player, owned the car. I was a junior in high school and had only been playing professionally for a year. We went to Bop City to sit in on the jam session. As

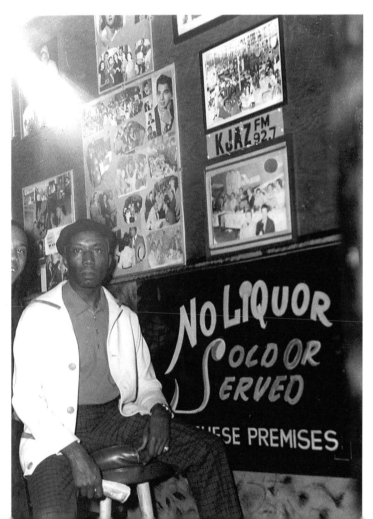

Jimbo in front of "No Liquor Sold or Served" sign. According to the musicians, most everyone found a way around this rule. *Steve Jackson Jr.*

we were waiting our turns, Paul Gonsalves, from Duke Ellington's band, got up on stage and began to play. He sat right next to me and played his heart out. And then, it was my time to speak. And apparently I did okay, because the next time I saw Paul, he remembered me and my playing.

Being in a place like Bop City, I began to realize that there were so many people who were innovators and fantastic performers on their respective instruments. It widened my scope, because the level of music was so high.

EARL WATKINS: You would go in the front door into a long room. The first thing you had to do was get past everybody because you knew everybody. Then in the back was the bandstand. Thursday night was Celebrity Night, so we would set up a big table and have a party for the

Bop City regulars. *Steve Jackson Jr.*

Flip Numez on piano at Bop City, 1950s. *Jerry Stoll*

celebrities who happened to be in town—Basie, Billie Holiday, Dinah Washington, Sammy Davis Jr., whoever happened to be in town.

STEVE NAKAJO: So all of a sudden, right in the heart of J-town, is this jazz club called Jimbo's Bop City, and it doesn't come alive until after 2 A.M. So if you were really hip in this community, and you really wanted to get exposed to certain things, you'd try to sneak out of your house and sit outside Jimbo's, because you were too young to go in, and be able to hear all the jazz that was going on in the club. And then at 6 A.M., everybody left and went to do their thing.

FEDERICO CERVANTES: A high school friend of mine named Duane wanted me to go to Bop City. He wasn't a musician, but he hung out with musicians. My father didn't want me to go because he thought Duane was going to be a bad influence on me, and I would be hanging around the wrong people. One day, while in the Fillmore, I ran into Duane. He said, "You know, you are just a few blocks from Bop City. Come on over and I'll show you the place." It was daytime, and I just looked in.

But then I started sneaking out at night, and one night I did go in with Duane. Jimbo had a house band— bass, drums, and, at the time, Stanley Willis was the piano player. I said, "I can do what he does, three times better." Jimbo said, "Yeah, get up here!" So Stanley sat down and I got up to play with the rhythm section and we swung and liked it. When Jimbo heard me play, he told me Stanley wasn't the pianist no more, and Jimbo wanted me to work. I told him I would because it was my chance to go out and get on the scene. So I began going down there seven nights a week, from 2 until 6 A.M.

I got on the recording map because of Bop City. I was working there during a local session when Chico Hamilton came in and played drums. We played until morning, and he stayed over two more days so we could play together again. He urged me to go down to Hollywood with him and he would introduce me to Richard Bock, owner of World Pacific Records. So I went and got a recording contract, thanks to Chico Hamilton.

EDDIE ALLEY: Bop City was one of the first places singer Johnny Mathis sang. He was from San Francisco—lived next door to us, and my kids came up with him. His family was so poor, and they lived in the house in the back. We were poor, so anyone who lived behind us was really poor! Now he's living in Rudolph Valentino's house down in L.A. and is a millionaire, and I ain't got a pot! But when he was first getting started, he sang with me a few times.

EARL WATKINS: Johnny Mathis was a track star, at Polytechnic High School, I think. At the same time, he was just trying to get started. At first, he was a rank amateur. He didn't know his keys and would jump the meter. But he had such a beautiful voice, and he was such a nice young man. The last time I saw him, he was playing in Chicago and he had a first-class show. He was on his way up, but he was still a sweetheart.

Johnny Mathis singing at Bop City early in his career, late 1950s. *Steve Jackson Jr.*

Jerome Richardson and Pony Poindexter, two of San Francisco's better-known jazz musicians in the 1950s. Richardson later moved to New York City to further his career. *Steve Jackson Jr.*

FRANK JACKSON: Frank Fischer had just got out of the army when he first came to Bop City. I met him that first night. He came in with an old-fashioned suitcase horn. The case was heavier than the horn! I was playing with Pony Poindexter that morning. Dexter Gordon was also on the set. If Pony saw a horn player come in, he'd call him up to play, and they'd always play something really fast and give the new guy a workout.

So when Pony saw Frank come in, he said, "Come on soldier boy, come up." Frank came up, took his horn out, and Pony called "Cherokee." They played the first chorus, and before anybody else could play, Frank was already playing the solo and played about three or four choruses. Nobody knew him, but it just woke the place up. He really burned it up. Pony was a little bit embarrassed,

because it was supposed to be a head-cutting session, and it backfired on him!

Pony was a good horn player, but he was cocky and egotistical, and devious sometimes, too. I knew sometime he was going to get it. A lot of times he'd burn up guys who came in by having them up there sweating with that tempo. Frank played that tempo like he wrote it. He was really something else. The other guys were laughing on the stand, and Frank didn't know what was going on. So he asked me, "What's the matter?" And I told him exactly what happened. He looked at me and laughed, because it never occurred to him!

Pony was one of our finer musicians. He traveled some. He went to Texas with Lionel Hampton and had to call Jimbo to get money to come back home! He blew all

Duke Ellington and Johnny Hodges at Bop City, 1950s. *Jerry Stoll*

Two couples at Bop City under a sign congratulating Duke Ellington, circa 1950s. *Steve Jackson Jr.*

of his money in Texas, and Hamp couldn't give him any money because his wife was handling his affairs. She had to do that because Hamp would give away the shirt on his back.

EDDIE ALLEY: I knew Pony Poindexter very well. He was down with the street life. He kind of went overboard with the dope stuff.

FRANK JACKSON: There was a drug scene, but I never got into it. I was motivated by fear. It wasn't just restricted to the musicians, but it caused personal problems for a lot of musicians because a lot of them lost their lives. Sad. A lot of them thought it would enhance their playing.

EDDIE ALLEY: They all wanted to be like Bird [Charlie Parker]. They had to have some heroin so they could sound like Bird.

JOHN HANDY: For me, it was all about the music. I didn't want anything to do with the drug scene, and I didn't go to Bop City to socialize. In fact, I don't recall ever sitting down and talking to anybody. I was always on the band-stand, playing, and then I left.

When I was twenty-two, after I had gotten out of the army and returned to San Francisco, I met this beautiful young lady at City College and asked her out. We decided to go to a couple of places before getting some food, so I took her to Bop City. I got up on stage to play and became so preoccupied with what I was doing, I forgot she was there! By the time I remembered, she had left. I wasn't being rude, but for me, the music was everything, and that's what I went there for. Needless to say, I never dated her again!

FRANK JACKSON: Teddy Edwards and I lived in an apartment building on Lyon Street, in the Fillmore. Teddy and Bird were good friends, and one night, when Bird was in town, Teddy brought him up to Bob City after his gig. He sat in with us, and it was fun. I got to talking with him. He was working downtown, I think at the Blackhawk at 66 Hyde. At that time I was working at Bop City six nights a week and did for about seven years.

You never knew who was going to come in. One night—well, it was really one morning—Coltrane was there. He was a young man, and he was doing something different from everybody else. They wanted to know what he was doing. What kind of horn he had. What kind of mouthpieces he used. What kind of reeds. And he was looking at them strange, like, why are they asking me all these questions? He was sort of a quiet guy, but he would answer the questions. He didn't feel like he was anything phenomenal. He was just a horn player. But he was quite a horn player.

Then there was Charlie Parker, who took jazz up a notch—from jazz to bebop. The Bop City musicians were blown away, and so was the audience. The response was just to listen and enjoy and try to understand what the

Publicity photo of Charlie Parker, 1950s.

Jimbo and famous San Francisco newspaper columnist Herb Caen inside Bop City. Caen was introduced to the Fillmore in the early 1940s by Vernon Alley, a former college classmate of Caen's. *Steve Jackson Jr.*

Musicians Frank Butler, Armando Peraza, and George
Walker inside Bop City, early 1950s.

musician was doing. You were right there, so you knew what they were doing. It wasn't like seeing somebody on stage. You were right there, with them.

A lot of local jazz enthusiasts were there every night. They didn't care who was playing. The audience would ask for a song, and if the band agreed on it, they would do it. It was pretty organized. Some people would play, then they'd let somebody else play and just sort of pass it around like that.

PHILIP ALLEY: I used to sneak into Bop City. I had an old hat I used to pull down over my head. But Jimbo knew who I was. He would say, "Go sit in the corner." I'd go sit there and wouldn't be able to drink anything because he knew who I was, and he knew my father and he knew my Uncle Vernon. So I had a little place where other kids couldn't go.

It seems like Jimbo's would be a big old place with a big stage, but it was very small, narrow, and tight. It would be packed, and the musicians would come in and out and play. There was no format. They'd just play all night long. One guy, he gets a solo, then he'd pack up his stuff and leave and somebody else would take his place. It was a heck of a place. Jumping!

I knew a lot of the musicians that were playing. Many times, they might have been in my house that day or the previous day because they were traveling through. So they'd play there and then they'd come by our house and eat. So I kind of got away with it, even though I was underage.

Bop City waitress holding the Jimbo's Bop City placard, 1950s.

PHILIP ALLEY: When I was young, the jazz musicians would come by all the time, and my mom would cook red beans and rice. Dizzy Gillespie would be sitting there eating, and Ben Webster, Sweets Edison, and all these musicians would be conversing, and I'd listen. They'd talk about life, about women that were crazy about them, and I heard all these things. I learned a lot about life by listening to these musicians. It was the real lowdown, the realistic life.

FRANK JACKSON: Lionel Hampton used to come into Bop City. Hamp would play piano. I'd play the chords and he'd play the top. He wanted me to go on the road with him, but I wouldn't do it.

Cousin Jimbo For Mayor

Louis Armstrong and his second wife in front of his
mural likeness on the wall of Bop City, 1950s.

ALLEN SMITH: Chet Baker was stationed at the Presidio playing in the Army band, and he'd come out to Bop City and jam with us whenever he could. He was a very nice guy. We hit it off and had a lot of fun together. Of course, he wasn't *Chet Baker* at the time! (laughs). He went on to become Chet Baker.

JOHN HANDY: Bop City was where I met Ella Fitzgerald. She was touring and came in with a big entourage. She knew Cousin Jimbo, so that's why she was there. I was part of the house band, and she got up and sang. She was so talented and so musically intuitive. Everyone wanted to get on that bandstand, and the easiest way was to sing. The bar was so low, but there were a few exceptions. Ella. Sarah [Vaughn], Carmen [McCrae]. They all got on the stage at Bop City.

ALLEN SMITH: You never knew who was going to be in Bop City. One night I was there and "God was in the house." That's an expression people used back then when Art Tatum walked into the room. He was the greatest pianist anyone laid eyes on. So one night I happened to be playing with a group of guys, and he came in. We asked him if he'd care to play, and he said, "Yeah, but I want to play with you guys." And we said, but we want to hear you! So he says, "Well, I tell you what. I'll play a song for you if you then let me play one with you guys."

So we traded off. And when it came time for his tune for us, we would sit down like little children at the edge of the stage, underneath the piano, looking up at him and watching him play every note! And of course, every note

Chet Baker in the audience at Bop City. Bobby, a local drummer, is behind Baker. In the late 1940s, in the army and stationed at San Francisco's Presidio, Baker would sneak out to play at the Fillmore clubs. Faking insanity, he was discharged and began his career as a musician, often returning to the Fillmore. According to Baker, he was in the Fillmore scoring drugs when he was jumped and all of his teeth were knocked out in 1968.

was a pearl as far as we were concerned. And then when he would finish, he would suggest a tune that we could all play together, and then we did. It was one of the most memorable nights I have ever spent at Bop City. The night God sat in with us.

PHILIP ALLEY: Various musicians would take turns playing, and sometimes they'd get to the point where they liked to blow each other off the stage. They'd have these battles. Jam sessions. One guy would blow the saxophone. Another guy would get up there and try to match him on his trumpet. It was very exciting. Hustling and bustle all the time. People and players in and out. All night people. All types would come into Bop City after 2 A.M.

ALLEN SMITH: Jimbo wouldn't allow any bad actors in the club, because it was a detriment to business. There was an expression of brotherhood there that existed among all peoples. You came there to enjoy yourself, and if somebody came on wrong in the racial sense, uh-uh! Within a minute people would confront the person and tell them, "You don't come in here and carry that racist attitude."

EARL WATKINS: Girls would come from out of town and naturally they'd want to hear jazz. So they'd come to Bop City, and the next thing you knew, they'd meet some nice well-dressed colored fellows. Even at some of the downtown clubs, things started to open up. I took many a girl down to Bop City just to show them the town. There weren't any problems that I know of.

JOHN HANDY: Nothing is like New York, musically speaking, but when you consider how small the African American population is in San Francisco, we did okay. There wasn't a Fillmore sound per say, but Dexter Gordon lived here for a while, Charles Mingus lived here. Jerome Richardson and Teddy Edwards lived here. Vernon and Eddie Alley and Pony Poindexter were from here. Chet Baker. Richard Williams. Richard Wynnes—all of them lived here for a time. We were young then. We didn't do too badly, but some of us felt we had to leave San Francisco and go to New York to help make their music scene great.

FEDERICO CERVANTES: I played at Bop City for ten years straight, and then on and off. I got a chance to experiment with chord progressions and things of that nature, even when I was playing behind the other musicians. But after a while, my excitement was not coming from the front line. Musicians coming in were too repetitive, trying to hog the whole show and trying to show each other, as well as the public, who could play like whoever was popular on record at the time. That's what bored me. I started working at other places. The first was when I got a booking in Chicago at the Blue Note. My time in the Fillmore seemed to be winding down.

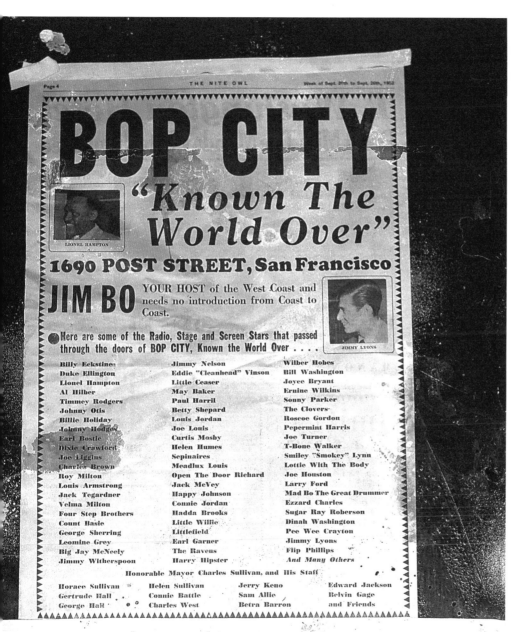

A poster in the window declares Bop City "known the world over," 1950s. *Steve Jackson Jr.*

L–R: **Skippy Warren, Carl Perkins, and Chico Hamilton on stage at Bop City, mid-1950s. According to some of the Fillmore musicians, Skippy was one of the few people who could master the Bop City bass.** *Steve Jackson Jr.*

Duke Ellington and friends feasting inside Bop City, 1950s. *Steve Jackson Jr.*

Jimbo inside Bop City, 1950s. The murals were created by Harry Smith (1923–1994), an experimental filmmaker, jazz painter, and creator of the famous recorded collection *Anthology of American Folk Music*. *Jerry Stoll*

A Bop City jam session with Arthur Prysock at left, Teddy Edwards on the right, 1950. *Steve Jackson Jr.*

A rare photo of a female sax player on stage jamming at Bop City, 1950s. *Steve Jackson Jr.*

Sammy Davis Jr. jamming on the bongos at Bop City, 1950s. Many famous Hollywood stars dropped by the nightclub when in town. *Steve Jackson Jr.*

Jimbo loved hosting parties and would often use Bop City during off-hours for celebrations. *Steve Jackson Jr.*

Max Roach with sunglasses and unknown group inside Bop City, 1950s. *Steve Jackson Jr.*

Frank Courtney drumming at a Bop City Jam session, 1950s.
Courtney was both a great drummer and fantastic dancer. *Jerry Stoll*

Group of patrons in front of a painting of musician Amos Milburn, corner booth
of the Texas Playhouse, 1836 Fillmore Street, September 10, 1958.

Chapter 3

END of an ERA

★★ THE FILLMORE ★★ AND THE WESTERN ADDITION, ALTHOUGH THRIVING, ⋯ also had their share of ⋯ PROBLEMS.

—

Willy Orey with painting of Ivory Joe Hunter, salvaged from the Texas Playhouse before it was torn down by the Redevelopment Agency. *Lewis Watts*

The housing stock, some of the oldest in the City, was beginning to fall apart after years of neglect due to the Depression, World War II, and the beginning of "white flight" to the suburbs. In 1948, the San Francisco Redevelopment Agency was created to "modernize" San Francisco, one of more than a dozen such agencies set up around the United States. The 1949 Federal Housing Act set aside federal money to rebuild the nation's cities, with an emphasis on demolishing the old and rebuilding the new. Between 1950 and 1970s, most major cities began redevelopment projects, most focused on poor, non-white neighborhoods.

San Francisco's Redevelopment Agency first set its sights on the old Produce Market, an area beleaguered by rats, disease, and filth. Dozens of blocks were cleared down to the dirt, replaced by the Embarcadero Center and Golden Gateway, a combination of housing, shops, and office buildings. It was an unmitigated success, bringing people and businesses back to an area once avoided by nearly everyone. Buoyed by the positive response, the Agency selected the Western Addition for their next extreme makeover. This time, however, things didn't go according to plan.

Newspaper articles and editorials as early as 1942 began highlighting what the authors saw as problems in the Fillmore and demanding that the area be redeveloped. Most had similar themes: that the housing in the Fillmore was falling apart, crowded, crime ridden, and filled with minorities. An April 22, 1942, editorial in the *Examiner* read, "Avert Slum Menace: City Should Act to Salvage Japantown," calling the area a "dreary 'Little Tokio [sic]'." The *Examiner*'s 1943 "Slum Expose" started off by telling readers about "Six Children in a Single Room" and introducing them to Joe and Pedro, two children who had just been released from Juvenile Hall. The article went on to say, "This area is also commonly known as the Fillmore District, now called by police 'Little Dead End'," and pointed out that the neighborhood had "a great number of races and nationalities." A 1947 *Examiner* article even proclaimed that city officials felt that they would see "eventual profit" once the Fillmore had been redeveloped.

Ironically, these articles and editorials were published during a time most Fillmore residents recall as being the best of their lives. While they agreed that the housing stock was old, they felt they lived in an exciting, vibrant, and economically thriving neighborhood; in short, a wonderful place to live. Fillmore residents knew that their neighborhood was being targeted for redevelopment, but they had no idea what to expect. However, some became concerned and began to speak out. A July 1948 meeting in the neighborhood's YMCA on Buchanan Street drew more than 300 concerned residents. Community leaders such as Dr. Carleton Goodlett, president of the San Francisco chapter of the NAACP, and Mrs. Michi Onuma, publisher of *The Progressive News*, spoke out against the redevelopment

The Owl Drug Co., 1601 Fillmore Street, looking west down Geary Street in 1952, before the street became the six-lane Geary Boulevard. The Redevelopment Agency painstakingly photographed every building on every block of the area slated for redevelopment, rating each building as "good" or "poor." Most buildings were marked "poor." By the late 1960s, nearly all the buildings in the photographs were demolished.

project, prophetically pointing out that "no guarantees have been provided that new housing built in the area will not be priced out of the range of the average worker living there," and that "scores of small businessmen would be wiped out by the plan."

Despite the protests, the first house in the Fillmore was demolished in 1953, kicking off "Western Addition Project A-1," what would become one of the largest redevelopment projects in the United States, encompassing hundreds of city blocks and impacting more than 20,000 residents. Two-lane Geary Street was excavated into a partially submerged, six-lane boulevard, so that residents of the Richmond District could get downtown more quickly. By the late 1950s, 4,000 residents had been moved from the area around Japantown in order to make way for the new "Japanese Culture and Trade Center."

In 1963, a second redevelopment plan for the Western Addition was announced. Phase A-2 encompassed nearly 60 square blocks, affecting more than 13,000 Fillmore residents. By now, with much of the neighborhood under redevelopment, many of the businesses and nightclubs began to move to other neighborhoods or to close, fulfilling the prophesy of the 1948 neighborhood meeting. Residents began to band together, creating WACO, the Western Addition Community Organization, in 1967 to fight against the displacement of the Fillmore residents by redevelopment, ultimately winning a lawsuit against the city to stop the wholesale demolition of the neighborhood. While the group won, in many ways it was too late, as entire blocks had been stripped of buildings, leaving the dirt lots that had fascinated me so much as a child. It would be nearly twenty years until the Fillmore Center, a combination of apartments and storefronts anchored by a major grocery store, would finally be built. By then, the neighborhood had been changed forever.

The last two of the original jazz clubs to close in the Fillmore were Minnie's Can-Do, which lasted until 1974, when it moved from Fillmore Street to Haight Street, and Jack's, which relocated from its original space on Sutter Street to several other spaces before ending up on the corner of Fillmore and Geary, across the street from the Fillmore Auditorium. It still exists as a nightclub, although it was bought by blues musician John Lee Hooker and a bevy of backers in the late 1990s and renamed the Boom Boom Room. It and Rasales' Jazz Club are the only two nightclubs to currently feature jazz, blues, and R&B, although the Redevelopment Agency has been trying to encourage other clubs to open up in what has been renamed the Fillmore Jazz Preservation District. The name seems ironic, since besides the Fillmore Auditorium, little remains of the neighborhood that once housed the Fillmore's jazz, blues, and R&B nightclubs, except for an incredible cache of memories and photographs that capture San Francisco's Harlem of the West.

The Congo Nightclub, 1718 Fillmore, looking south to the Bank of America on the corner of Fillmore and Post Street, circa late 1950s. The Congo is in the space formerly occupied by the Havana Club. The Bank of America building is one of the few original buildings left in the Fillmore. It currently houses a Goodwill Thrift Store.

View of the 1700 block of Fillmore Street, circa 1950s, showing the Esquire Barber Shop, a clothing store, and the Congo nightclub.

Jack's of Sutter, in the street-level space of the Victorian at right, mid-1950s. This group of Victorians was demolished, and brown shingle condominiums currently occupy the space.

An early 1960s promotional photo from the San Francisco Redevelopment Agency showing a Fillmore resident in new, modern housing that was built in the neighborhood.

St. Mary's spiritual service in the Fillmore, 1950s. *Steve Jackson Jr.*

Bell's Clothes, Champagne Supper Club, and Don's Café on the 1800 block of Post Street, October 1952. The Club Alabam was on the same side of the block, just a few doors to the left of Bell's Clothing.

Wesley Johnson Jr.'s Pharmacy, 1960 Sutter Street, between Fillmore and Webster, late 1950s. All that is left of the pharmacy is the stone entranceway, which now serves as the entrance to condominiums rebuilt on the space.

GallenKamp's Super Stores, 1698 Fillmore Street, October 1952. Just a tip of the building that housed the Dog House Bar can be seen in the far left corner of the photo.

Wesley Johnson Sr.'s Club Flamingo and Exclusive Hotel Texas, 1836 Fillmore Street, mid-1950s.

Tanners Korean Restaurant / Breakfast Club, formerly the Plantation Club, 1628 Post Street, late 1950s.

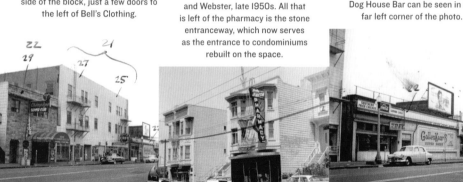

FEDERICO CERVANTES: When I came back to the Fillmore, there were some other piano players on the scene, but I wasn't impressed with them. Jimbo let me come back whenever I wanted, but a lot of places, like the Plantation Club, had closed. Bop City and Jack's of Sutter were the only ones left. I think integration started it, being able to go into the clubs where you couldn't go before, or you could play there but you couldn't go in through the front door or sit down. A lot of the players who had been around for ten years or more started getting into drugs. Plus, the Redevelopment Agency started tearing down a lot of the apartments. Because of all of this, a lot of African Americans were leaving the Fillmore.

FRANK JACKSON: Starting in the late 1950s, a lot of musicians left the Fillmore clubs to tour or go to other cities. In order to get anywhere as musicians, you had to. Then you could come back as headliners in the bigger clubs around town. Jerome Richardson got disgusted. He was getting work, but he couldn't advance. You couldn't get any recognition in San Francisco. Jerome told me, "Frank, I'm moving to New York." Richard Wynnes left here for the same reason. They left here together, and they did big things. Their careers took off.

Redevelopment destruction, looking down Fillmore Street, mid-1950s.

A large Victorian apartment building, February 1952, later demolished.

The Grand Café was at 1801 Post Street, in the heart of today's Japantown. All the buildings in this 1952 photo are no longer there.

EARL WATKINS: It was very traumatic to see it all go away. We all made a living playing music, and all we did was play our music, and then it was gone. I don't know why you would think this, but you kind of think it's going to go on forever.

STEVE NAKAJO: When redevelopment began, the vibrant community I knew, my friends, my whole world, started to change. I used to look down the street and see nothing but Victorians. And then, at one point, you'd leave in the morning and there would be a bulldozer parked in front of some buildings, and by the time you came back from school, the houses weren't there anymore. Block by block, gone. Totally leveled.

The relocation camps took almost everything away from the Japanese community, and then to be able to hold it all somehow while you're at camp, then come back after the war and reestablish yourself just to have the Redevelopment Agency come and declare eminent domain and take away your house? Incredible!

Demolition to make way for the new Japan Trade Center, known today as Japantown, mid-1950s.

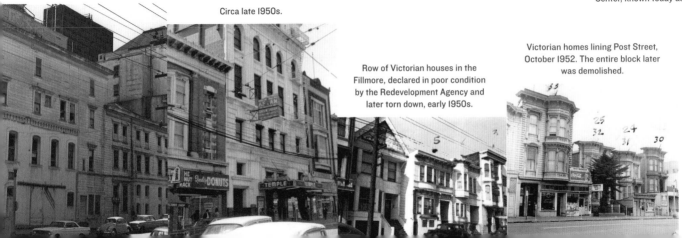

The California Brewing Co. building, late 1950s.

Circa late 1950s.

Row of Victorian houses in the Fillmore, declared in poor condition by the Redevelopment Agency and later torn down, early 1950s.

Victorian homes lining Post Street, October 1952. The entire block later was demolished.

MAYOR BROWN: I think that the people who wanted to redevelop the Western Addition saw the commercial value of the space. It was centrally located; the dividing line between downtown and the Avenues in every sense of the word. I think they saw land and they had to clear the land, and the only way to clear the land was to use the tools of government to achieve that goal. You look at the results and it does appear to be "Black Removal," but I think the motivation was pure commercial greed. But it was devastating to the Black community. The churches began to lose populations. The black businesses, which had been viable, wonderful, and productive, were totally destroyed. The entertainment world for African Americans virtually ceased to exist in San Francisco. The great life that was Harlem-ish for us was destroyed by the redevelopment process. It was a blow to African Americans. A blow from which we frankly have never really recovered.

PHILIP ALLEY: There were a lot of reasons the Fillmore dried up. The government took a lot of people's property through eminent domain. They took the whole strip of Geary Street, the building where Bop City was. Leola King had a great loss. They wanted to redo the area, and she wasn't included. A lot of people were supposed to come back and they never did. It's not the same Fillmore. It's the Black people that had the businesses and clubs on the Fillmore, and they've all gone. It's changed completely.

Inside Bop City, circa 1950s. The wallpaper was later replaced with colorful murals. *Steve Jackson Jr.*

A couple enjoying themselves at Bop City, 1950s. *Steve Jackson Jr.*

Getting hair processed, late 1950s.

Also, musicians had been playing in venues that the average person could afford, and then the musicians began playing at very expensive clubs for white people, so that eliminated the neighborhood audience, because they couldn't afford it.

Before, when Black musicians came into town, they would play for the white audience downtown and then come to the Fillmore and really get down. I mean, they'd let it all hang out and do their own thing, because they were surrounded by their own. It was a beautiful time. It was an era in the past. But that's life. Things change. Move on. And hopefully the new jazz clubs going in might bring a little life back to the Fillmore.

BOBBIE WEBB: It makes me very sad to see what has happened in the Fillmore. Most people can't afford to live in the neighborhood anymore. Redevelopment tore down everything and keeps saying that they are going to put in affordable housing, but affordable for whom? And calling it a Jazz District! I know what was here, and it wasn't just a jazz district, it was an R&B and blues district. They are using the word *jazz* because it lends the neighborhood prestige. Draws in people with money. The word *blues* scares people. It makes people think of bad things. The people who lived in the Fillmore a long time are being phased out. They don't want people like us here.

Jimbo with his waitresses and the Post and Buchanan signs, which is the
intersection where Bop City was located, 1950s. *Steve Jackson Jr.*

Singer on stage with Jimbo Edwards,
Bop City, late 1950s. *Steve Jackson Jr.*

Bop City, circa 1950s. *Steve Jackson Jr.*

Vaudevillian performer "Bicycle" in front of the New Fillmore Theater at 1329 Fillmore Street, 1950s.

STEVE NAKAJO: You ever get into a situation where sometimes your mood is gray? And everything is overcast, cloudy and gloomy? You know, riding the 22 Fillmore bus through the neighborhood during redevelopment was like that. Dark and empty. With all of these skeletons where buildings once stood, and others boarded up, ready to be torn down. Dismal and desolate, all the way up Fillmore Street. And the only spots of people on the street were at bus zones.

JOHN GODDARD: Redevelopment came and tore down all the record stores and barbecue places. You bet I remember it, because they tore everything down. It got to the point, around 1965, where I didn't feel safe coming to Fillmore Street anymore. It was the beginning of the

Black Power Movement, and people were angry—rightly so. But I didn't feel comfortable. Nothing ever happened, but it was a different vibe. I quit going out to the clubs in the Fillmore. The neighborhood had changed. It was really too bad, because it was the end of an era for me.

DAVID JOHNSON: There is a bad side to gentrification, when you destroy a neighborhood. In Europe they preserve their cities and buildings, but in America we tear them down. The neighborhood is not coming back. This city has totally changed. It's in the hands of real estate companies. It could never be what it was. I think I would prefer it to remain as a memory, and you can visit it in terms of the images.

Robert Lee, a well-known figure in the Fillmore, at left in white cowboy hat, mid-1950s.

Little Robert Lee's birthday cake, early 1950s.

JOHN HANDY: By the mid-1960s, the interest in jazz fell off. Black people's tastes changed, and so did white people's.

ALLEN SMITH: It is pretty hard to turn back the clock. There have been too many changes. The anxieties don't exist that used to exist. There isn't a need for Blacks to have a place where they can relax and enjoy themselves, escape the sting of racism and have a chance to mingle with other races without fear. You might say, these days, who needs a Bop City to go to? Along the path of history, there have been some good times, along with some horrible, bad, horrendous times. There are many things that still are not what they should be in our society. But can you repeat history?

FEDERICO CERVANTES: I can't say that jazz in the Fillmore will be what it used to be. I don't think it will ever come back the way that it was when it was basically African American. But the Fillmore was a real good musical education for me. Without that I don't know in which direction I would have gone. I loved classical music, but I never made that my goal. I saw myself through Oscar Peterson. Duane and Bop City. Fatso Barry and the Ellis Theater. Being able to play at Leola King's. All of this gave me my jazz education.

FRANK JACKSON: Redevelopment closed the clubs. Took away businesses. Put people out of work. They were in a hurry to do it, and then they didn't do anything. No development. Nothing. They had no intentions of developing anything for us.

JIM MOORE: Before redevelopment, the Fillmore was a neighborhood. When your musicians weren't working, they would go to jam sessions and create. And when you went to a session, if, say, a trumpet player played a certain type of line, and you were a trumpet player, you'd want to do something better than he did when you'd go back. One thing would feed off the other. It wasn't about money—it was about creating. That's one of the things that caused the elimination of the art form. Now it's all big corporations. Corporations have come in, and the bottom line is the dollar. In those days, we had control of the music to a certain extent. Like Charles Sullivan. He was a promoter, and he understood it wasn't just about the money. He enjoyed the music, too.

Toward the end of the '50s, people lost jobs and weren't working as much as they were during the earlier days. Then Bill Graham came on the scene, and rock ended up having a larger white audience than Black. So things just started to go downhill.

Chef and waitress behind counter of unknown
Fillmore restaurant, 1950s.

Flyer for Willie Mae "Big Mama" Thornton at the Both And,
350 Divisadero Street, 1950s. As the clubs began to close in the Fillmore,
Divisadero Street took over as a hub for jazz, blues, and R&B.

SUGAR PIE DESANTO: Oh, man, if I could turn back the hands of time. I would like to go back myself to the old days of the Fillmore. Yes, ma'am.

JIM MOORE: I wish I could go back. Just to listen to those sounds. Go back and visit the clubs and catch a set at the Blue Mirror and hang out at the Texas Playhouse and Jack's, the Booker T., the hotel, just go in and catch Ben Webster. You could go to any club, and everybody was a pro and they did good shows. You could just sit there and forget about your problems.

SUGAR PIE DESANTO: Yeah, your troubles would just melt away. The music brought us together, and everybody was happy and smiling. People weren't jumping up trying to fight.

JIM MOORE: Oh, man, people have no idea. They have absolutely no idea what it was like. And what it did for you. The Fillmore was one of the most exuberating and fun times in my lifetime. The Fillmore was something else.

Dancing in a Fillmore flat, late 1940s or early 1950s. *David Johnson*

Local DJ Uncle Tiny at the microphone with
Eddie Alley on drums, inside an unknown Fillmore
nightclub, 1950s. *Steve Jackson Jr.*

The 4 Naturals. *L–R*: Delmare Smith, drums; Sammy Simpson, sax; Frank Jackson, piano; Eddie Hammon, bass, 1950s.

JACK McVEA and his ORCHESTRA
Exclusive BLACK & WHITE Recording Artists

"OPEN THE DOOR, RICHARD"

EXCLUSIVE MANAGEMENT
Reg. D. Marshall Agency
HOLLYWOOD, CALIFORNIA

Jack McVea and His Orchestra promo photo, late 1940s. The band had a hit with the song "Open the Door, Richard."
Signature reads: "Wesley opens the door to success, much luck, Wes, Jack McVea."

THE
FILLMORE
NEIGHBORHOOD MAP

A

PINE ST

BROADERICK ST

DIVISADERO ST

SCOTT ST

PIERCE ST

STEINER ST

WILMOT ST

FILLMORE ST

WEBSTER ST

COTTAGE ROW

BUSH ST

SUTTER ST

POST ST

GARDEN ST

GEARY BLVD

O'FARRELL ST

BEIDMAN ST

ELLIS ST

HAMILTON
RECREATION CENTER

RAYMOND
KIMBALL
PLAYGROUND

AVERY ST

① ② ③ ④ ⑤ ⑥ ⑦ ⑧ ⑨ ⑩ ⑪ ⑫ ⑬ ⑱ ⑲ ⑳ ㉑ ㉒

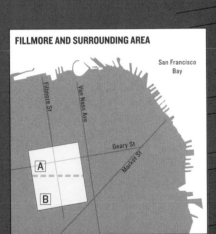

FILLMORE AND SURROUNDING AREA

San Francisco
Bay

Fillmore St

Van Ness Ave

Geary St

Market St

A

B

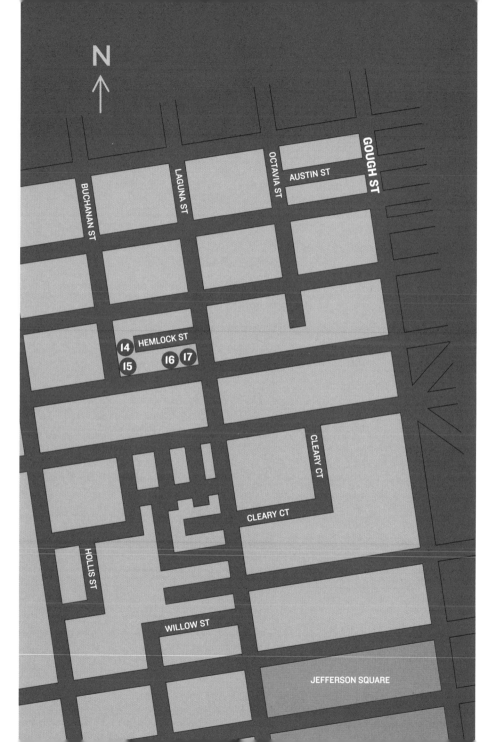

FILLMORE CLUBS, BARS AND LANDMARKS

Although many addresses housed different clubs over the years, only the ones mentioned in the oral histories have been listed below. Included are additional key Fillmore landmarks that can still be seen in the neighborhood.

LEGEND

★ Open Venue | Existing Structure
● Closed

1. **Minnie's Can-Do**, 1915 Fillmore Street (p. 83)
2. **The Encore/Big Glass Bar** 1801 Fillmore Street
3. **Texas Playhouse/Club Flamingo**, 1836 Fillmore Street (p. 96)
4. **Town Club**, 1963 Sutter Street (p. 82)
5. **Elsie's Breakfast Nook/Harold Blackshear's Café Society**, 1739 Fillmore Street (p. 91)
6. **Havana Club**, 1718 Fillmore Street (p. 137)
7. ★ **Marcus Books**, 1712 Fillmore Street
8. **Club Alabam**, 1820A Post Street (p. 80)
9. **Jack's Tavern/Jack's of Sutter**, 1931 Sutter Street (p. 76)
10. **The Long Bar**, 1633 Fillmore Street (p. 94)
11. ★ **The Boom Boom Room**, 1601 Fillmore Street
12. **New Orleans Swing Club/The Champagne Supper Club**, 1849 Post Street (pp. 84–89)
13. ★ **Fillmore Auditorium**, 1805 Geary Boulevard (p. 126)
14. **Vout City/Bop City**, 1690 Post Street (p. 138)
15. **Jackson's Nook**, 1638 Buchanan Street (p. 93)
16. **California Theatre Club Restaurant**, 1650 Post Street (p. 134)
17. **Plantation Club**, 1628 Post Street (p. 130)
18. **The Bird Cage**, 1505 Fillmore Street
19. **Booker T. Washington/The Edison Hotel**, 1540 Fillmore Street (p. 131)
20. **Ellis Theater**, 1671 Ellis Street (p. 116)
21. **Bal Masque Ballroom**, 1641 Ellis Street
22. **Aloha Club**, 1345 Fillmore Street

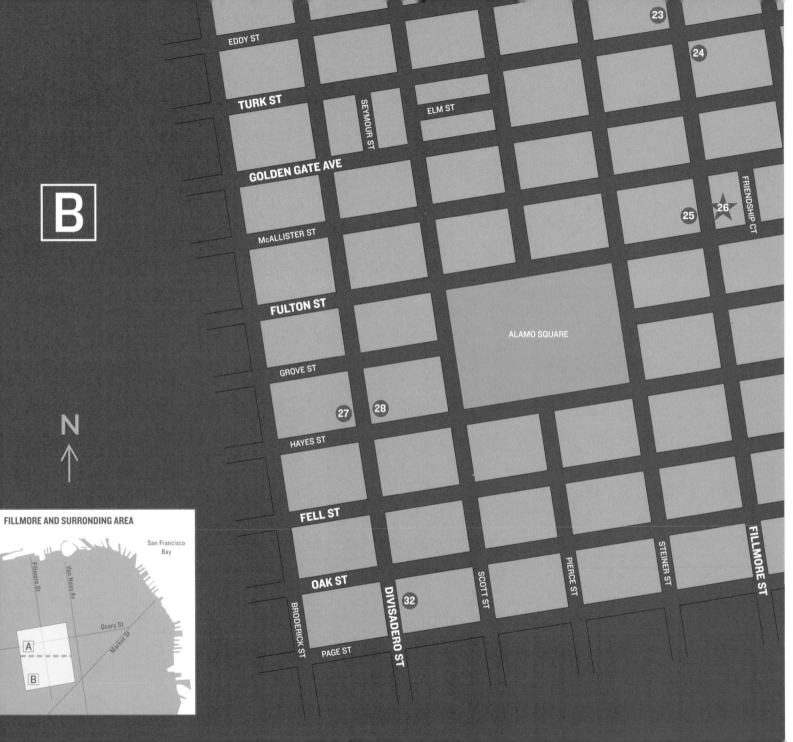

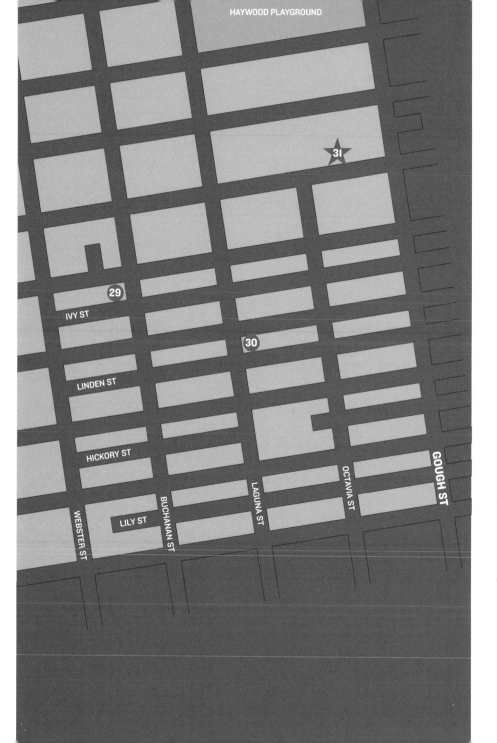

HAYWOOD PLAYGROUND

★ 31

29
IVY ST

30

LINDEN ST

HICKORY ST

WEBSTER ST

LILY ST

BUCHANAN ST

LAGUNA ST

OCTAVIA ST

GOUGH ST

LEGEND

★ Open Venue | Existing Structure
● Closed

㉓ **Sportsman's Inn,** 621 Divisadero Street
㉔ **Primalon Roller Rink,** 1223 Fillmore Street (p. 118)
㉕ **Blue Mirror Cocktail Lounge,** 935 Fillmore Street (p. 110)
★㉖ **Old Muni Substation,** 1190 Fillmore Street
㉗ **The Bird Cage,** 1505 Fillmore Street
㉘ **The Half Note,** 628 Divisadero Street
㉙ **Manor Plaza Hotel,** 930 Fillmore Street
㉚ **Dottie Ivory's Stardust Club,** 597 Hayes Street
★㉛ **African American Cultural Complex,** 462 Fulton Street
㉜ **Both And Jazz Club,** 350 Divisadero Street

SELECTED BIBLIOGRAPHY

Books and Articles

Angelou, Maya. *I Know Why the Caged Bird Sings*. New York: Bantam, 1983. First published 1969 by Random House.

Broussard, Albert. *Black San Francisco: The Struggle for Racial Equality in the West, 1900–1954*. Lawrence: University of Kansas Press, 1993.

Bryant, Clora, Buddy Collete, William Green, Steven Isoardi, Jack Kelson, Horace Tapscott, Gerald Wilson, and Marl Young, eds. *Central Avenue Sounds: Jazz in Los Angeles*. Berkeley: University of California Press, 1998.

Chamberland, Carol P. "The House That Bop Built." *California History Magazine*, 75, no. 3, 272–283.

Cogdell DjeDje, Jacqueline, and Eddie S. Meadows. *California Soul: Music of African Americans in the West*. Berkeley: University of California Press, 1998.

Daniels, Douglas. *Pioneer Urbanites: A Social and Cultural History of Black San Francisco*. Berkeley: University of California Press, 1990.

Fine, Doris. *When Leadership Fails: Desegregation and Demoralization in San Francisco Schools*. Berkeley: University of California Press, 1986.

Flamm Jerry. *Good Life in Hard Times: San Francisco's '20s and '30s*. San Francisco: Chronicle Books, 1978.

Hamlin, Jesse. "Jazz Helped Break the Color Barrier: Blacks and Whites Mixed Freely in San Francisco Clubs." *San Francisco Chronicle*, February 8, 1998.

Ichioka, Yuji. *The Issei: The World of the First Generation Japanese Immigrants (1885–1924)*. New York: Collier Macmillan Publishers, 1988.

Issel, William, and Robert Cherny. *San Francisco, 1865–1932: Politics, Power and Urban Development*. Berkeley: University of California Press, 1986.

Kazin, Michael. *Barons of Labor: The San Francisco Building Trades and Union Power in the Progressive Era*. Champaign: University of Illinois Press, 1989.

The Legend of Bop City, VHS. Produced and directed by Carol P. Chamberland. San Francisco: Red Sable Productions, 1998. www.buyindies.com

Levy, Harriet Lane. *920 O'Farrell Street: A Jewish Girlhood in Old San Francisco*. Berkeley: Heyday Books, 1996.

Neighborhoods: The Hidden Cities of San Francisco: The Fillmore, VHS. Producer, Peter Stein, Elizabeth Pepin, associate producer. San Francisco: KQED-TV, 1999.

Oaks, Robert F. *San Francisco's Fillmore District*. Chicago: Arcadia Press, 2004.

Okazaki, Suzie Kobuch. *Nihonmachi: A Story of San Francisco's Japantown*. San Francisco: CA SKO Studios, 1985.

Robles, Al. *Rappin' with Ten Thousand Carabaos in the Dark: Poems*. Los Angeles: University of California Press, 1996.

Pepin, Elizabeth "Swinging in the Fillmore: A Look Back at San Francisco's BeBop Era." *San Francisco Bay Guardian*, February 25, 1998.

Scott, Mel. *The San Francisco Bay Area: A Metropolis in Perspective*. Berkeley: University of California Press, 1985.

Stoddard, Tom. *Jazz on the Barbary Coast*. Berkeley: Heyday Books, 1982.

Whiting, Sam. "Farklempt in the Fillmore: A Few Traces of Jewish History Remain for Those Who Know Where to Look." *San Francisco Chronicle*, July 18, 2004.

Wirt, Fredrick M. *Power in the City: Decision Making in San Francisco*. Berkeley: University of California Press, 1974.

Yoshida, George, *Reminiscing in Swingtime: Japanese-Americans in American Popular Music, 1925–1960*. San Francisco: National Japanese American Historical Society, 1997.

ACKNOWLEDGMENTS

Web Sites

All About Jazz
www.allaboutjazz.com

Amacord's Fillmore Jazz Project
www.amacord.com/jazz

The Boom Boom Room
www.boomboomblues.com

*Neighborhoods: The Hidden Cities of
San Francisco: The Fillmore*
www.pbs.org/kqed/fillmore

Fillmore Jazz Preservation District
www.fillmorejazz.com

Fillmore Street Jazz Festival
www.fillmorejazzfestival.com

Jazz Now
www.jazznow.com

*Jazz West: Celebrating the
Best in Bay Area Jazz*
www.jazzwest.com

*Musicians Union Local Six:
The Bay Area Musicians Union*
www.afm6.org

Rasselas Jazz Club on Fillmore Street
www.rasselasjazzclub.com

San Francisco's Fillmore Street
www.fillmorestreetsf.com

Village Music
www.villagemusic.com

Musician Websites

Sugar Pie DeSanto, Jim Moore
and Jasman Records
www.jasmanrecords.com

John Handy
www.saxworx.com/handybio.htm

Vince Wallace
www.vincewallace.com

Wayne Wallace
www.walacomusic.com

Bobbie Webb
www.bobbiewebb.com

Marie Browning of the San Francisco
    Redevelopment Archives
Carol Chamberland
Chuck Collins
Dr. Dan Collins
Darryl Ferrucci
Fillmore Auditorium Staff of the 1980s
Greg Garr
Carolyn Herter
Rupert Jenkins
KQED-TV
Vanessa Kulzer
Ken McCarthy
Ben Pease
San Francisco History Room staff of the Main
    San Francisco Public Library
Peter Stein
Professor Jill Stoner
Bob Stuber
U.C. Santa Cruz Arts Research Institute
U.C. Santa Cruz Committee on Research
University of California Institute for Research
    in the Arts
Michael Willis

Special thanks to Alan Rapp and Steve Mockus,
who have the patience of saints!

And all the residents, former residents, and
musicians of the Fillmore

INDEX